$100M
Money Models

How To Make Money

ALEX HORMOZI

What People Have Said About Alex Hormozi

"Alex is my husband." - Leila Hormozi

"I have known many people, Alex is one of them." - Friends of Alex

"Alex does things I have seen." - Alex's dad

"Alex is better at some things than others." - Alex's mom

"Alex wrote a book. I have read many books." - Magazine critic

$100M
Money Models

How To Make Money

ALEX HORMOZI

Disclaimer

The information provided in this book is for educational and informational purposes only. The author, publisher, and licensed distributor have made reasonable efforts to ensure that the information within was accurate at the time of publication. The author, publisher, and licensed distributor make no representation or warranties with respect to the merchantability, fitness for a particular purpose, current or continued accuracy or completeness, and reliability of the contents of this book.

The strategies, tips, and tools discussed in this book are the author's personal opinions and are provided as-is. They are intended to provide helpful and informative material on the subjects addressed in this book. Success in any marketing and business endeavors is based on a wide range of factors unique to each individual or business.

Laws are subject to change and may vary by location and jurisdiction. You, as the reader, are encouraged to consult with a professional where appropriate and review the current local laws before implementing any marketing strategies or campaigns.

Earnings and income representations made by the author are aspirational statements only of your potential earnings. The success of the author and others referenced herein, testimonials, and other examples used are exceptional, non-typical results and are not intended to be and are not a guarantee that you or others will achieve the same results. Individual results will always vary and your results will depend entirely on your individual capacity, work ethic, business, skills and experience, level of motivation, diligence in applying the strategies discussed, the economy, the normal and unforeseen risks of doing business, and other factors within or beyond your control.

No guarantee is made that you will achieve any result at all from the ideas in this book. The author, publisher, and licensed distributor disclaim any representations or warranties (express or implied), including, without limitation, those of merchantability, fitness for any particular purpose, current or continued accuracy or completeness, and reliability. Reliance on the information provided is solely at your own risk. As further described herein, the author, publisher, and licensed distributor shall in no event be held liable to you or any party for any direct, indirect, punitive, special, incidental, speculative, or other consequential damages arising directly or indirectly from any use and/or misuse of this book, which is provided "as is", and without warranties.

As always, the advice of a competent legal, tax, accounting, finance, or other professional should be sought and obtained.

Any statements that express or involve discussions with respect to predictions, goals, expectations, beliefs, plans, projections, objectives, assumptions or future events or performance are not statements of historical fact and may be "forward looking statements." Forward looking statements are based on expectations, estimates, and projections at the time the statements are made that involve a number of risks and uncertainties which could cause actual results or events to differ materially from those presently anticipated.

Running a business involves the risk of loss as well as the possibility of profit. All businesses involve risk, and all business decisions remain the responsibility of the individual. The author, Bumble IP, LLC, Acquisition.com, LLC, and their affiliates (collectively referred to herein as the "Company") have not

Guiding Principles

"Risk comes from not knowing what you're doing." - Warren Buffett

"More important than the will to win, is the will to prepare." - Charlie Munger

A Quick Word

LEILA:

I wrote this dedication seven years ago in my first book…

I want to thank my partner, my ride-or-die, Leila. You found me at my absolute worst, and you have fought beside me shoulder to shoulder ever since. You said you would sleep with me under a bridge if it came to that, and I have never forgotten. You stood tall when everything was crumbling around me. I would go to war with you. I would die for you. If the world were a hurricane, standing with you is like being in the eye, calmly observing the storm raging around us. There's no one else I'd want by my side to fight the battles that come. Being with you makes the stars look within reach. Here's to a life filled with the impossible.

And seven years later…nothing's changed.

TREVOR: *As iron sharpens iron, so one person sharpens another. Proverbs 27:17*

It's a rare and wonderful thing to have the smartest man you've met call you a friend. If ignorance is the only true evil, and knowledge, the only true good, you, my brother, are a force of good. The world is better with you in it. And I will fight to keep it that way. My life wouldn't be the same without you. I wouldn't be the same without you. I doubt I will ever be able to repay the favor you have given me by being in my life. But I'll live trying. Thank you for giving me a gift far more than a paragraph at the beginning of a book can ever repay. We will put our brick in the wall. Here's to a once in a generation friendship. Philia.

Contents

START HERE

*The world breaks everyone and afterward many are strong
at the broken places. - Ernest Hemingway*

Where I slept at my first gym: my "concrete bedroom."

I stared at the ceiling in the dark, alone. I had no one to go to. It sounds cool when you tell the story later, but it didn't feel that way. I was terrified.

I went against my father's wishes. I skipped out on business school. I spent all my savings. Everyone I cared about told me not to do it. I was the idiot that gave up on a good career.

I thought I would look forward to the struggle. But, it got real…*fast*.

Kids partied all night in the parking garage above me. They'd race over the steel dividers. It sounded like gunshots echoing in my concrete bedroom. And as soon as I started to pass out, I'd get jolted awake by another *bang-bang bang-bang*.

I finally gave up trying to sleep at night. I settled for midday naps—in the utility closet. Then, in the dead of night, I worked. *I had to make money.*

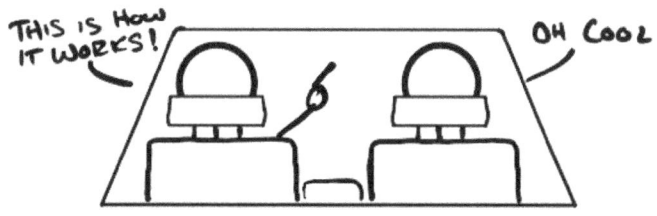

My gym sat across the street from a large storage unit business. The owner became one of my few members…only out of convenience. A few weeks after he joined, he pulled me aside after his workout. "I've been doing a little math," he said, "It looks like you're struggling." I tried to hide my embarrassment, but I failed. "Alright kid. Let's grab breakfast tomorrow." I hesitated, thinking about my bank account. Before I could answer, he said "…don't worry. My treat." Relief.

The next morning we met at the local diner at around 5 AM.

As the waitress brought our coffee, he asked "How much time you got left to live?"

"Huh?"

"How much cash you got saved up?"

"About five grand."

"How much time does that give you before you run out?"

I thought about it for a moment. "About a month."

"Tough. How you getting customers?"

"I have a $39 six-week special on a discount site."

"How many customers have you gotten?"

"Four."

"Looks like you've got a problem…that you need to solve…fast." He let his statement sink in. Then I saw a grin spread across his face. "Let me ask you a question… *How much does a free month of storage cost?*"

I shrugged…"Uh, nothing?"

He took note of my confusion and said "Alright, let's go for a ride. I'll explain it at my facility."

As soon as we walked in, the girl at the front desk greeted us. "Good morning, gentlemen!"

"Good morning, Judy. *How much does a free month of storage cost?*"

"$127 sir," she replied cheerfully.

He smiled and he turned to me. "Wanna know how?" I nodded. He took me through the office and down one of the rows of freshly painted units. "So, we advertise the first month as free, *and it is.* But what's the first thing you need after you get a storage unit?"

"I don't know."

"Exactly. Nobody really does. But I do—and I help 'em out. So let me give you a hint…" He pointed towards the lock on the door.

"Right…a lock!"

"Yea, and not one of those flimsy locks kids use on their lockers. Those won't fit anyway. Besides, any goon with bolt cutters can get through 'em in a second…but not one of these bad boys." He tapped the lock to emphasize his point.

"Yeesh, it looks like it. Where do you even get one of those?"

"Funny you should ask. *I've got a whole storage unit full of them.* Yours today for just $47 bucks."

"Okay, okay…I get it. They come in for the free month but what good is a storage unit unless you can lock it?"

"Exactly," he said.

"I get it, so where does the other $80 come from?"

"Great memory. So, what else are you gonna want?"

I shrugged.

"Well, if you have *stuff* to store. You're gonna need *boxes* to store it in! But, never fear. We've got boxes with tons of different shapes and sizes to fit all your storage needs. We also offer tape, labels, and heavy duty markers to make sure you know exactly what's in every box and where you put it. Super handy."

"Oh, duh. That makes perfect sense."

"What else are you gonna need?"

"I don't know…help moving it?"

"Yes! Now, we don't actually offer in-house moving services. But, we have an affiliate relationship with a local moving business and make a kickback. And if you want to move all the stuff yourself, that's fine too. We have dollies, hand trucks, straps and other useful tools available…*for a fee*. After all, why buy a bunch of stuff you'll only use once? What a waste!"

"Oh yea, didn't think of that."

"What else are you gonna want?"

"Uh, I really don't know."

"Well, what you store is valuable, right? At least, valuable to you in some way. I mean, if it wasn't, you'd send it all to the dump! So…you're gonna want some insurance in case something bad happens. Now, I already give $500 of free insurance to all customers. But if you have one of the special locks *only I offer*, I'll bump it to $100,000, for only an *extra* $10 per month." He puffed up with pride.

"Dang. And all that adds up to 127 bucks?"

"Yep. But, we're not done yet. You know what always seems to happen?"

Onto his game now, I played along. "Beats me, what happens?"

"Everyone has way more stuff than they think. And they *always* rent too small of a unit! In fact, it happens so often we *always* offer one size up. They get the space they need and we make a few extra bucks. It works out for everyone."

"Wow. This is pretty cool. I didn't know any of this stuff."

"Of course not. Why would you?"

"Fair enough. But how can I use this to grow my gym?"

"Yeah. I've been playing this game as long as you've been alive. And when you figure out how to make money in one business, and I mean really figure it out, you see ways to make money in any business. And one thing's for sure. The longer you play, the more you learn."

"Wow, so you've had this place for 23 years?"

"This place, no. This one is one of my newer locations."

"You have more than one?"

"I have 27."

"Oh…crap." I felt two inches tall.

"Anyways, I gotta get to work. You know your way out?"

"Yea," I chuckled. "I think I can make it across the street."

2.5 years later . . .

I now had six gyms. I had leveled up. And I wanted to level up again. So I paid $25,000 for an hour of time with a famous marketer. I had never spoken to him. But I knew his stuff like the back of my hand. I had one goal for this call—for him to help me scale my gyms.

After brief introductions, we dove in.

"...so, yeah, and that's how I open my gyms at full capacity on day one. I put $3,000 down for a lease and run a few day's worth of ads. I sell customers in the empty building. Then the cash from those sign-ups goes toward more ads, equipment, paint, flooring, furniture, signage, and whatever else the location needs. Doing it this way, I've opened up a new location every six months with no debt."

"Wow—so cool! Explain it to me in a bit more detail, would you?"

His business was making a million bucks a month. Those numbers blew my mind. *And he wants to hear how -I- advertise?* I beamed with pride.

"I advertise a Free 6 Week Challenge until I get about 20 leads per day," I said.

"Got it, keep going," he said.

"About half the leads show for appointments. I sell half of those who show into a $600 program. So about 25% of my leads become paying customers. I also get another $80 in profit per customer from supplement sales. Not too shabby."

"Agreed," he grunted. "So you make like 680 bucks per customer before you even open your doors. Pretty dang good…but you left something out."

"What did I leave out?"

"How much you payin' per lead?"

"Oh…$5." *If a deafening silence ever happened in my life—this was it.*

He stuttered a bit, "So you put *one* dollar in…and get *34 dollars* out…*in 48 hours?*"

"Yeah? Is that good?"

"It's amazing," he said. "Do you have anything happening on the back end?"

I grinned ear-to-ear. "Yea! A few weeks later, I tell them they can get their $600 back as credit if they choose to sign up for a year. Two-thirds of sign-ups convert into memberships. So I end up with a full gym and $20,000 of monthly memberships…for $3,000 down. Then I rinse and repeat."

"Wait a second, you do all this *in thirty days?*"

"Yep. Pretty cool right?"

He rubbed his eyes. "You shouldn't be running gyms."

Oh god. I thought he was going to compliment me—but he told me I should quit? My mind raced…

"Alex," he said, snapping me back to reality, "you have a level-10 skill in a level-2 opportunity."

Well, at least he doesn't think I suck. "Ok, what should I do?"

"You shouldn't be running gyms. You should be showing other gym owners how to do what you just showed me."

I hated the idea of giving up on what I took years to build. But…he made *a lot more money* than I did. I figured, if I ignored his advice, I may as well burn my money. So, I took his advice.

***

Over the next nine months, I closed down my newest gym and sold my other five. That gave me the time to go all in on my new company: Gym Launch. Over the next two years, I flew around the country turning gyms around. Then, after 30+ turnarounds, I switched to a licensing model. I no longer flew out in person. Instead, I helped them follow our proven model to fill their gyms and increase profits. A small market to be sure, but they were *starving*—some literally. But once they filled their gym in thirty days, they told their friends. Gym Launch took off like a rocket. It was wild.

Over the next five years I took over $43,000,000 in owner distributions. Then, I sold 66% of the company at $46,200,000 in an all-cash deal. With that deal, I crossed a $100M net worth at age 31. And to be clear, no one was more surprised than me.

From there, my wife and I founded our family office Acquisition.com to invest in businesses we know how to grow. Our portfolio at the time of this writing does over $200,000,000 per year in annual revenue. It spans brick & mortar chains, software, services, and ecommerce. Even though we work in many different industries, our companies all grow using the same principles I share in this book.

So What's In It For You?

In a few pages, I took you from sleeping on the floor to crossing $100,000,000 in net worth. So the natural question is…how? Answer: *by making more money from customers than it costs to get them.* And that's what this book *$100M Money Models* is all about.

Since I've been in business, the landscape has changed more than once. And it'll keep changing. The good news is, sound principles help you print money no matter what. I've learned a lot of Money Models. I cover my favorites here.

$100M Money Models shows <u>already proven</u> offers you can use <u>today</u>. And, the instructions to make them happen. Think of *$100M Money Models* as a book of winning lottery tickets—all you have to do is cash them in.

Also, I want to make something clear, *these are my private notes.* If it's here, I've made money with it. These chapters contain my observations and experiences with different businesses. From local chains, to physical products, to services, education, software, and so on. And they were scattered everywhere over the years. *Until now.*

<u>This is my cookbook for making money.</u>

How This Book Is Structured

This book teaches you *one* insanely profitable thing: **how to build a $100M Money Model.** With a $100M Money Model, *you make so much money in the first thirty days that the cost of getting more customers will never be a problem again.* With so many customers, you'll be forced to work on *everything else* in your business to just keep up! A problem for another book to solve (winky face).

<u>Book Outline</u>

Start Here: *You just finished it.*
Section I: What's a Money Model? *Coming up next…*
Section II: Attraction Offers
Section III: Upsell Offers
Section IV: Downsell Offers
Section V: Continuity Offers
Section VI: Make Your Money Model

That's it. Easy peasy. Let's get to it.

Pro Tip: Faster, Deeper Learning By Reading & Listening At The Same Time

Here's a life hack I stumbled on a few years ago. If you listen to an audiobook and read the physical book or ebook at the same time, you read faster *and* remember more. You store the contents in more places in your brain. Nifty stuff. This is how I read books worth reading.

I also do both because I struggle to stay focused. If I listen to the audio while reading it helps me avoid zoning out. It took me two days to record this book out loud. I did it so if you struggle like me, you don't have to anymore.

If you want to give it a try, go ahead and grab the audio version and see for yourself. I've made my books as cheap as the platforms let me, so this isn't a ploy to make some extra coin—I promise. I hope you find it as valuable as I have.

I figured I'd put this "hack" early on. This way you'd have a chance to do it if you found the first chapter valuable enough to earn your attention.

Pro Tip: Hack For Finishing Books

I get distracted easily. So I need little tricks to keep my attention. This one helps me alot: Finish chapters. Don't stop in the middle. Completing a chapter gives you positive reinforcement. It keeps you going. So, if you meet a tough chapter, finish it so you can start fresh on the next one.

SECTION I: WHAT'S A MONEY MODEL?

"Hormozi has the highest return on advertising of any business using our advertising tracking platform...by a mile. He has the biggest discrepancy we've seen between dollars spent and dollars earned. And we only work with businesses spending at least $250,000 per year on marketing or more, so these are the cream of the crop marketers and his numbers are in the stratosphere by comparison." - Alex Becker, CEO, Hyros.com

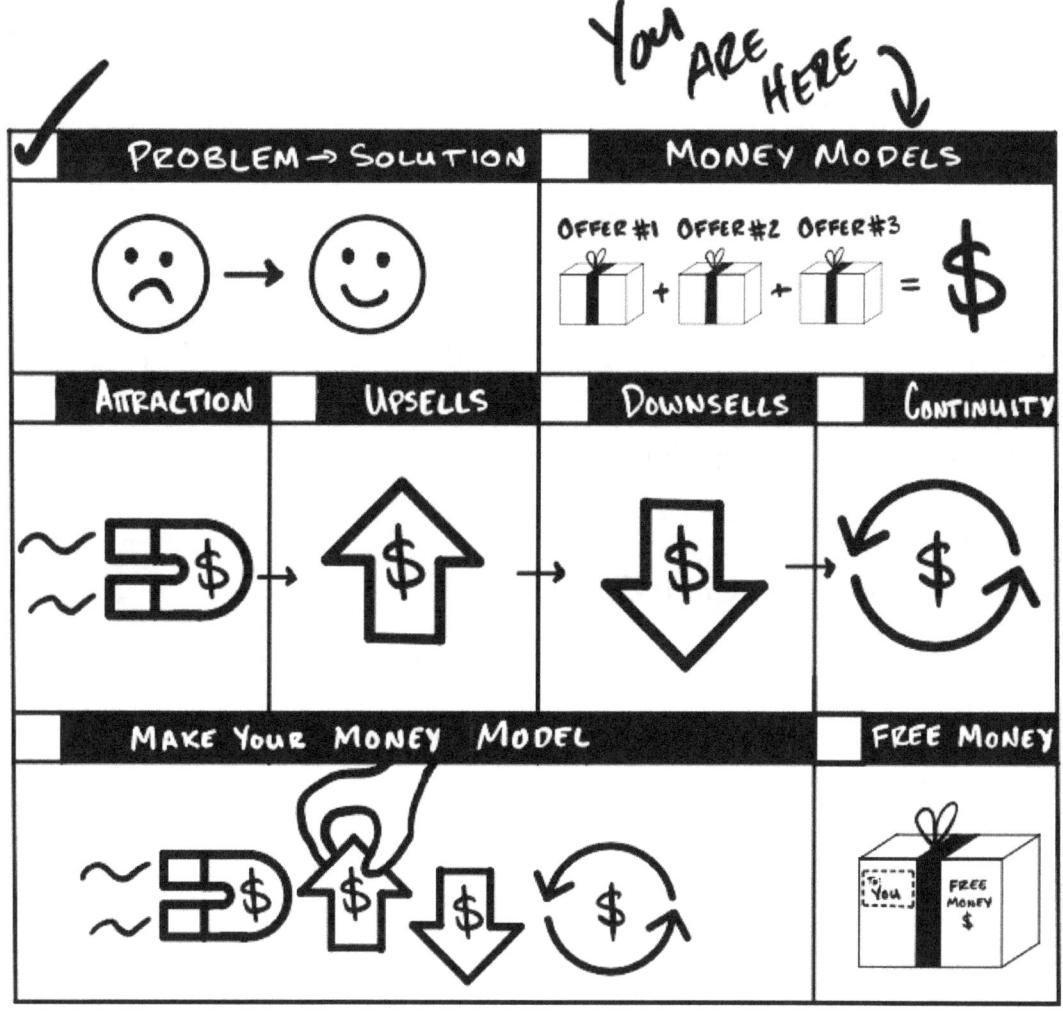

December 2019.

"Hello sir, can I have your ID so I can look up your reservation?" the car rental agent said, smiling. I already had my ID ready and slid it across the counter.

"Hmm. It looks like we don't have the car you reserved. We have an equivalent car though… but you're a big guy. Would you prefer a roomier pick-up truck instead?"

"Yea, that sounds nice," I said.

"I've got you down here for three days." She cocked her head to the side a bit. "Would you like to have a late return so you can turn in the vehicle at any time during the day without worrying about late fees?"

I pulled up my schedule on my phone. "Yeah, we have an evening flight. So that sounds good."

"Great. Give me a second…just putting that in. So would you like better insurance to cover any bumps or scratches on the car? It covers any and all damage to the vehicle during your time."

"Nope I'm good. No plans on drag racing while we're here," I joked.

"So only the *minimum* insurance then?"

"Yep. That's all I'll need."

"Okay then, I'll have your keys in a second. Did you want us to take care of fuel so you don't have to worry about filling it up? You can return it on empty and not worry about paying a fee. We do it for $3.75/gallon."

"What's the gas around here?" I asked.

"About $3.50/gallon," she replied cheerfully.

"Sure, why not. I hate filling it up when I'm rushing to catch a flight."

"Alrighty then! Here's your receipt. Just go around the corner and your truck should be about halfway down on the left. Enjoy your trip!"

***

As I walked away, I glanced at the receipt and it stopped me in my tracks. I could only laugh at myself. I came for a $19/day car and I left paying $100/day. A 5x difference! And that's the power of a well designed Money Model. They knew everything I wanted (and things I didn't even know I would want). And when they offered them to me, I happily bought them.

A Money Model Happened

A Money Model is a *sequence of offers*. At their core, we find every opportunity to solve a customer's problem…and then offer to solve it. For that reason, Money Models tend to have many offers in a specific order. If you offer the right thing when customers realize they need it, you can make *as many offers as you like*.

This is the rental car company's Money Model stated plainly:

<u>Offer #1</u> Vehicle Upgrade

<u>Offer #2</u> Late Return

<u>Offer #3</u> Premium Insurance

<u>Offer #4</u> Minimum Insurance Downsell

<u>Offer #5</u> Prepaid Gas

So yeah, I paid more, *but it also solved more problems.* Let's break down the problems she solved:

- She solved my 'big man in a small car' problem by *offering* a vehicle that had more space.

- She solved my 'late checkout' problem by *offering* the flexibility to keep the vehicle longer.

- She solved my 'worries about dinging the car' by *offering* insurance to protect against it.

- She solved my 'risk of missing my flight' problem by *offering* a way to prepay for the gas ahead of time so I wouldn't have to do it on my ride back.

    …And all those things cost money *I was happy to pay.*

The rental car company thought out every nuance. They told me about the problem, then *made their solution available to me.* They offered solutions for higher fees and hassles I might have had later for smaller fees in total *right now.*

As a result, my $19 rental became a $100 rental. I paid *more money faster.* And now, we can see why the car rental industry brings in billions in the United States alone…*per month.* A successful Money Model.

Beware: Bad Money Models Kill Businesses

It costs many businesses more to get somebody to buy a thing than they make in profit off the thing. In other words, they lose money getting new customers—*that's a big problem.*

And here's what happens…

- They spend money to get customers.

- At the end of the month, they realize they spent more than they made.

- They cut back on advertising.

- Get fewer customers than they can handle because they can't afford them.

- Then, cut advertising altogether.

- Float the business with personal cash, loans, credit, and then…*pray* for profit.

- Sell percentages of their business just to keep the lights on.

- Wait months (or years!) to make their money back…if ever.

- Fall further and further behind until…

- Finally, they lose it all.

But it doesn't have to be that way. There's plenty of money. You just have to *go get it.*

In traditional business, the slow drip of profits from lots of customers *eventually* pays for a *single* customer. This 'drip' starves the business of cash. It means they can only get lots of customers through advertising…*if they already have lots of customers!* Big companies (or small companies with investors) can do this because they have the money to burn.

Think about it this way. If you spend $100 in advertising to get a customer and make $500 in profit from them, that's a great deal. You should take it all day. But what if it takes you two years to make your cash back? It's a great business…if you already have tons of cash in the bank. Otherwise, *you're gonna run out of money.* That leaves you with two options:

Option #1: Wait two years to get paid and pray you don't run out of money.

Option #2: Get paid fast and grow as much as you darn well please.

A good Money Model is option 2.

Author Note: Make Enough Profit To Cover Your Costs In 30 Days Or Less

I like to cover my costs of getting a customer within 30 days. Main reason: any business can get interest-free money for 30 days in the form of a credit card. If you clear your balance before the end of the month, it works just like normal money. So you can use credit to get a customer, pay it back, and then use it again to get the next customer. And if you can pay it off *before* the 30 days, you can go do it again. Rinse and repeat.

Good Money Models Make Millionaires

If you make more offers, and people buy them, you make more money. If you make more money, you can use it to get more customers. If they pay you that money faster, the faster you can get those customers *and* stay profitable.

But what if you make your customers twice as valuable, you get twice as many of them, and get those customers at twice the speed?…*your business grows 8x faster.* And if you triple them…*your business grows 27x faster.* See where I'm going with this? You can get really big, really profitable, really fast…*with just a few changes.* And that's exactly what I'm gonna show you how to do.

Next Up

Money Models are a sequence of offers. Different offers solve different problems. So if you want to win, you have to figure out what to offer *next*. To figure that out, you've gotta understand *The Four Offer Types…*

The Four Types of Offers That Make Money Models

Stop being poor. - Paris Hilton
The limit does not exist. - Lindsay Lohan, Cady Heron in Mean Girls

Making one offer works better than making none. And making more offers works better than making one. Combining offers in a sequence makes a Money Model. My Money Models combine four different offer types.

Four Types of Offers

There are four types of offers: Attraction Offers, Upsell Offers, Downsell Offers, and Continuity Offers. All improve our Money Model, but they all do it *differently*. They work great on their own, but together they make your business unstoppable.

1) **Attraction Offers** turn strangers into customers.

2) **Upsell Offers** get people to spend more cash.

3) **Downsell Offers** get people to say yes when they would have said no.

4) **Continuity Offers** keep people buying.

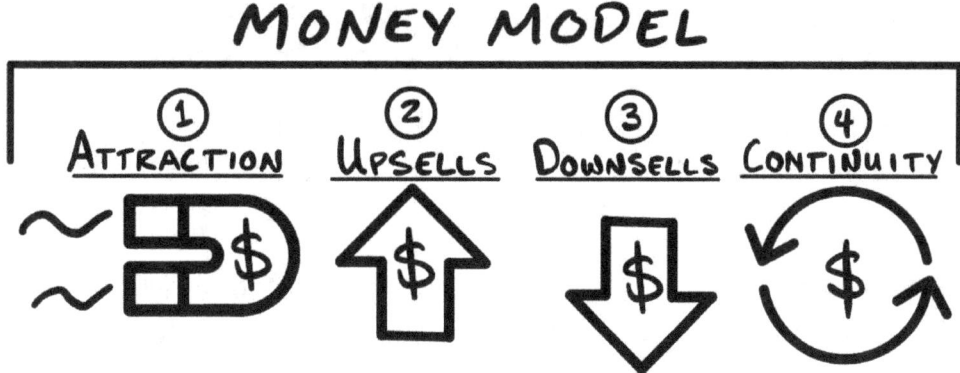

If you look at great businesses, you'll see different versions of these offers as core components of their money-making engine. You can use one, two, multiples of one, or all four together. You can combine them however you want. But, when I look at *my* most profitable businesses, I used all four. And here's why:

If you don't have an offer for getting customers, you won't get as many. But let's say you do. If you only have that one thing to offer, you won't make nearly as much money as you could. So if you have something to offer next, an upsell, you'll finally get some cash.

But, you still won't make as much as you could because lots of people will still say "no." So, we turn those "nos" into "yeses" with downsells. And that works fine. But it would be even better if you had that extra cash *guaranteed* to come in *month after month*. So, you make a continuity offer to top it off. That's how I like to do it.

How I Structured The Sections

I start with Attraction Offers, because if you're not getting customers, you need one of those first. Then, we cover Upsell Offers, followed by Downsell Offers. Then to finish the four types, I show you my favorite Continuity Offers *exactly how I learned them*.

How I Structured Each Chapter

Each chapter has six elements:

1) **Doodle** directly from my notes. Exactly as I drew it. It helped me remember it, so it will help you remember it, too.

2) The **story** of how I first learned this Money Model.

3) A **description** of how the Money Model works.

4) A few **examples** of how this Money Model works in different industries. Think of how you could use the Money Model in your business.

5) **Important notes** and tactics that make the Money Model work. These tidbits help you execute the play—like it's your hundredth time doing it—*on your first try.*

6) A **summary**. All the important points about the Money Model. Plus, some extra thoughts sprinkled in about how to make the Money Model more profitable.

Important Notes:

Alright. Before I release this pile of gold nuggets I need to make a few things clear:

1) **All Businesses Have Money Models. It Makes A Business A Business.** Switch the *poor person* mantra "this won't work for my business" to the *rich person* mantra "how will I make this work for my business?" They all work. *Be creative.*

2) **Some Money Models Work Better In Some Businesses Than Others.** They're just different ways to offer stuff. If you just try to copy what "they" do you'll be disappointed. To make it work for your business, you have to design your own (but don't worry, I'll show you how).

3) **If A Customer Asks For Their Money Back—*Give It Back.*** Avoid the headache. And if you made a goof—*fix the goof.* Don't be a silly goose. Treat customers well. Next time, spend the time and resources to get better customers.

4) **Hard Selling Is For Weak Products.** If someone doesn't want something, *that's OK.* Don't convince someone against their will. Make offers available at the time your customer has a problem and you'll be ahead of the competition. If they don't want it, no sweat. Find somebody who does. It's a numbers game.

5) **Obey The Law.** I learned these plays in different situations from different people using different platforms, in different times, in different places, following different rules. Advertising laws change all the time. And they tend to only get tighter—especially when it comes to "free." Check with lawyers to see if an offer you want to make is legal or not. This book is intended to be Money Model inspiration. Use it that way.

6) **Be Transparent.** State the facts. And if the facts aren't compelling, change reality to make them compelling or learn to frame them in a way that is. Don't lie. You'll short-change yourself long-term. And unlike credit card debt, you can't file bankruptcy to erase a bad reputation. Once you have a bad one, it sticks for life.

7) **Any Offer Can Be Used On Its Own, At Any Time, in Any Order.** A business works as long as it makes a profit. Most offers in this book could meet that minimum requirement *on their own.* When used in the right sequence, and at the right time, they make a *$100M Money Model.* I've got big dreams, and I bet you do too. So, we're gonna use 'em all.

With that said, let's go for a ride.

First Up: Attraction Offers

Most businesses spend too much to get customers and make too little from them. *They are cash-constrained.* But, you use cash to get more customers. And I like more customers. So I always solve this first with an Attraction Offer.

FREE GIFT: Bonus Tutorial On The Four Types Of Offers

If you want a more in depth look at how we think through layering different offers, go to acquisition.com/training/money. It's free and publicly available. My goal is to earn your trust. And trust is built brick by brick. Allow this training to be the first of many bricks. Enjoy. You can also scan the QR code if you hate typing.

SECTION II:
ATTRACTION OFFERS

How to turn eyeballs into money.

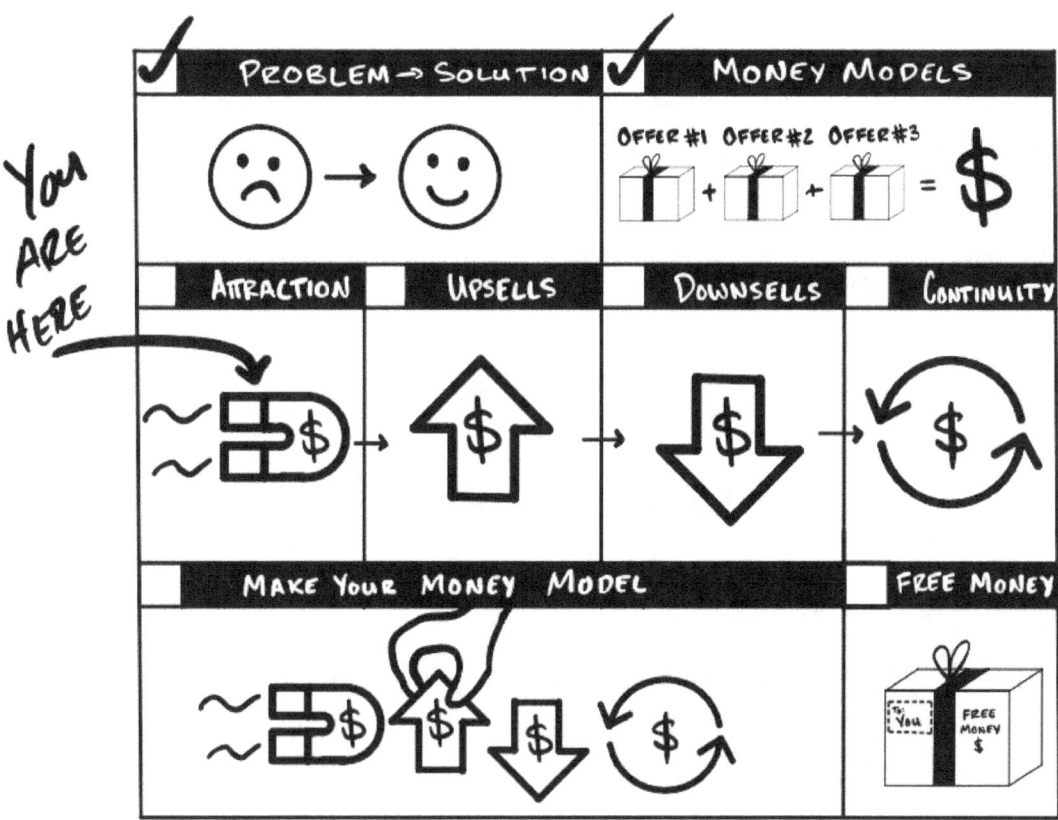

Attraction Offers generate leads *and* convert them into customers. They turn advertising into money by offering something free or at a discount. We do this because everyone wants a great deal. In a great deal, customers get *far* more value than the price they pay. Strangers can only take your word on the value. But, they absolutely understand the price. For that reason, discounts make *anything* a great deal to just about *anyone*. And, the greater the discount, the better the deal. The greatest discount of all being *free*.

So first off, any time I say "free" you can also use "discount" or "$1." Any time I use "discount" you can also use "free" or "$1" and so on. They exist on a continuum because they all discount a product to some level—even if you discount it by 100%!

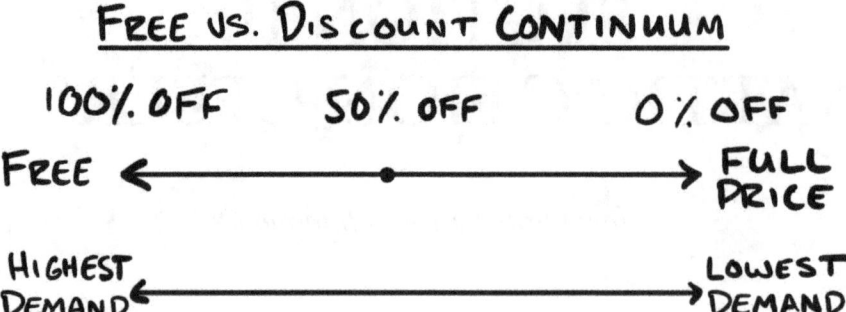

If you can imagine a way to use a discount or a free offer...then you can do it. After that, I'll let you use your noggin to exchange them as you see fit.

So How Do You Make Money By Offering Free Stuff?

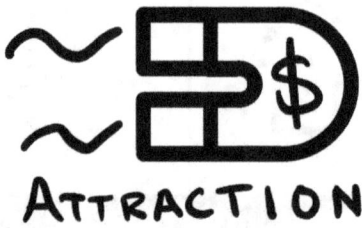

Think about it this way—people look for one thing and then buy another by accident *all the time*. Attraction Offers get them to do it *on purpose*. But what's a better deal than free stuff? *More and better free stuff.* One free thing is awesome. Two free things are awesomer. And, maybe to get those two free things, *they have to buy one*. That's how we make money on free stuff.

In this section, I go over my five favorite ways to make money by offering free stuff:

1) Win Your Money Back

2) Giveaways

3) Decoy Offer

4) Buy X Get Y Free

5) Pay Less Now or Pay More Later

Let's make some money.

FREE GIFT: Bonus Tutorial On Attraction Offers

I made a free video for you on how attraction offers work. If you want it, just go to acquisition.com/training/money. There's no opt-in required. Enjoy. You can also scan the QR code if you hate typing.

Win Your Money Back

If you do x within y time within z rules, you can get it free.

June 2013.

I was in a room full of experienced gym owners, and I was the new guy. We all took turns talking about what was working well. That's when Danny piped up.

"Yea…so as you guys know, I've been struggling with sales…and I think I got it figured out. I had this pain in the butt guy who wouldn't buy *anything*. He knew he needed it but he also said he needed more accountability. So we were going back and forth, and finally he came up with this idea. He said, *'How about this: I give you $500. You train me for eight weeks. And if I hit my goal, I get my money back. But in return, you can use my results to market your business. Fair enough?'*"

"So…what happened?" I asked.

Danny replied, "I figured he wasn't gonna buy anyways, so I sold him."

"Okay, so what happened with the guy?"

"He hit the goal."

"So did you give him his money back?"

"That's what you'd think, but he ended up using the money to buy more training!"

"Seems decent enough. What about marketing his results?"

"Dude, marketing his before and after pictures brought in *thirteen* referrals!"

"That's insane. Now we're talking."

"Yea, I know. I offer this to everyone now. The results are way better and people love the offer. And all the free advertising they do for us gets their friends and family to join too. I'm making more money than ever."

***

This is the first time I ever saw an offer like this. I updated it over time, but the core stayed the same: *pay now with a chance to get your money back later.* I used it for private training, group training, private nutrition coaching, and group nutrition coaching. Once I saw how well it worked with my current customers, I started putting the offer in my ads for new customers. My cost of getting customers went *way* down and my leads exploded!

Description

A Win Your Money Back Offer works like this. *You* set a goal for the customer *and* tell them how to reach it. If they reach it, then they qualify to get their money back *or* get it back as store credit.

This offer grew my gyms better than any other. It was also the first Grand Slam Offer that Gym Launch taught to gym owners. It has tons of flexibility. So if you want to get more cash, get more customers, and get them better results. Nothing beats it.

To 'Win Your Money Back' the person has three options: Get Results, Take Actions, or both. And to make this work, you have to make the <u>results</u> and <u>actions</u> *simple* to track.

<u>Results</u>: Here, no matter what they do, if the customer gets the result, they win their money back. For example: Making $X a month, Getting Y customers, Losing Z lbs etc. *Basically, they bet on their own ability to reach the goal.*

<u>Actions</u>: Here, you hold them accountable for *doing* actions instead of *getting* results. No matter what results they get, if the customer does what you ask, they win their money back. For example: attend all sessions, calls, meetings, log progress, take pictures, do assigned homework, etc. *Here, they bet on their ability to follow directions.*

<u>Actions</u> *and* <u>Results</u>: Here, you hold customers accountable to following directions and getting results. If they do both, they win their money back. Often, people wanting to achieve a goal have too few skills to do it. Even if they did bet on themselves, they'd fail. By setting a good goal for them *and* showing how they reach it, they have a fighting chance. *Here they bet on their ability to follow directions and that your directions will get them the result.*

Bottom Line: Customers put money down. If they do the stuff OR they get the result OR both—*they get it back as cash or store credit.*

Examples

Business To Consumer Offer: Free 28-Day Blueprint

Deposit X dollars and get it all back if you:

- ☐ Attend all your consulting calls.

- ☐ Post your progress in the group once per week.

- ☐ Journal daily in our app.

- ☐ Attend your feedback session and your transformation session.

  (Hint: calls and meetings become opportunities to make more offers.)

Business To Business Offer: 5 Customers In 5 Days Free Challenge

Deposit X dollars and get it all back if you:

- ☐ Send 100 messages per day.

- ☐ Report stats on messages sent.

- ☐ Attend daily training.

- ☐ Post finished homework in the group.

- ☐ Attend the day 5 consulting call.

  (Hint: here you offer more, better, or new products and services.)

Physical Product Offer: Put 1,000,000 Miles On Your Car, And Get A Free Car

Get a free car if you:

- ☐ Buy a new car from us.

- ☐ Drive the car 1,000,000 miles.

- ☐ Turn it in.

- ☐ Take pictures and be in a press release.

- ☐ We'll credit all your original purchase price towards your next car.

  (This was an actual offer.)

Important Notes

This offer has generated over $1 billion in sales industry-wide. It works. I have made a lot of money with it. You can too.

Win Your Money Back Works With New, Current, *And* Previous Customers. I like to use it with new customers because it offers the steepest discount possible—100%. I like it with current customers because it mixes them in with new customers. And I like to use it to get previous customers back because bigger incentives get them to come back.

It Works Well With Stuff People Start And…Quit. Like starting businesses, learning new skills, losing weight, building fitness, beauty regimes, self-care, time management, mental health management, etc. It keeps motivation during the early pains of learning. To this day, I have never seen a better way of setting up a program for results—a true win-win.

Don't Worry. This Offer Makes Money. If you did give all the money back, this offer wouldn't make money—*but it does*. First, many won't qualify—even with realistic conditions. Second, those who *do* qualify often stay as customers. But they can only stay customers *if they have something else to buy*. So have an upsell ready to apply their winnings (Section III).

Only Offer "Win Your Money Back" If You Feel Ok With Giving Money Back! Refunds are a part of doing business. However, when advertised well, the Win Your Money Back offer gets tons of extra customers. And when you give satisfied customers a great follow-up offer, *you make plenty of profit*. This more than outweighs the refunds. From the data we've collected from thousands of gyms, about 10% of all customers will ask for their money back. If you can't stomach it, don't do this.

Offer Store Credit Instead of Cash. If you don't want to offer cash back, you can offer store credit instead. My testing showed offering store credit and cash back got the same number of customers. So you might as well offer store credit. But, if you still want to advertise it as 'free,' pair it with an <u>unconditional satisfaction guarantee</u>. Adding the unconditional guarantee never materially affected the number of people who wanted their money back. Check with legal counsel in your area.

Don't Take Blood Money. If someone doesn't want me to have their money, I want it less than they do. As a personal rule, if a customer asks for a refund—entitled or not—*I give it to them.* Just focus on getting the next customer.

How To Create Your Win Your Money Back Criteria. These criteria make or break this offer. Good criteria have three characteristics:

1) Easy To Track. Train them on *exactly what they need to do* (or they will mess up). Bonus points if people already do it. Ex: Phones already track steps. Word processors already track word count. Cameras automatically date photos.

2) Gets Customers Results. Make criteria likely to get them their desired results. *Realistic* criteria do just fine. If you think the criteria look too easy, you've probably gotten *close* to realistic. They may take a few tries to get right, but so does anything else worth making. Ex: attend meetings, workouts, watch videos, etc. Whatever stuff the best customers do to get the best results, make *everyone* do it (and they'll get great results too).

3) Advertises The Business. Make advertising the business part of your criteria. For example: posting about their participation, tagging in social media, referring, or leaving reviews and testimonials.

How You Apply Store Credit [IMPORTANT]. When customers win their money back, offer to apply it over a longer period or to a bulk package. Just offer to apply it to something that costs more than their winnings. In my experience, this keeps customers engaged and makes you more money. Here's what that looks like:

- You have a product or service that costs $200 dollars per month.

- A customer wins $600 of credit. <u>Avoid</u> giving them three free months *up front*.

- Instead apply the $600 over 12 months → ($600/12 months = $50/mo discount).

- They now pay: $200 per month—$50 discount = <u>$150 per month</u>

- To be clear, they can use credit however they want. But, I recommend you present this first. If they ask to use it up front, you can share my experience—people fall off if they don't pay *something*. A discount over the long haul keeps them engaged over the long haul. So it's in the customer's best interest to keep some skin in the game.

- In-depth details on this Upsell Offer are in the Rollover Upsell chapter (Section III).

All Meetings And Calls Provide Opportunities To Make More Offers. Make check-in meetings part of your money-back criteria whenever you can. And make all meetings required to win their money back. Beyond helping them succeed, they are the best opportunities to make upsell offers. So after you've checked in, offer what makes sense based on their feedback. The Win Your Money Back Offer and my gyms had three appointments:

- Nutrition Orientation → "Before pictures"→ I make a supplement offer.

- Progress Check-in → I make a membership offer.

- Transformation Feedback → "After pictures"→ I make the membership offer again.

  o If they bought the membership at the last meeting, I offered a discount if they prepaid for a year.

Make Everyone A Winner. Promote and sell the program as though they will only get it back if they meet the criteria. But, about halfway through, make your next offer *as if they already won.* You lower the customer's anxiety about failing *and* you'll keep them longer. They'll also love you that much more. Something like:

I know you're trying to hit this short-term goal, but what's your long-term goal?...okay that's great to hear. You get that it's not about this program but about your long-term results. Tell ya what, to show you how much I want you to hit that long-term goal, I'll credit this program toward the next one whether you hit the short-term goal or not—how's that sound?"

At The End Of The Program, Let The "Losers" Win. If someone refuses your first upsell *and* fails the challenge, you can *still* upsell them again. Here's how: <u>act like they won.</u> I say something like:

"Don't worry about it. You started. That's the biggest victory of all. And even though you didn't hit your short-term goal, you met <u>ours</u>—which was finishing what you started. To show you that we're in this for the long haul, we'll credit your entire deposit towards staying with us long term. That way you get your money back and we can still hit your goal. How does that sound?"

You'll turn that frown upside down and they'll love you for it. Remember—<u>we don't get customers to make a sale, we make sales to get customers.</u>

The Win Your Money Back Offer Has A Simple Structure With Lots Of Flexibility. At its heart, you offer a product or service and a way for customers to get their money back if they actually use it. Then, if they use it the way you suggest, they will get good enough results and stay open to more offers and/or longer term commitments.

Summary Points

Win Your Money Back is magical for businesses that require their customers to put in continuous efforts to get their ideal outcome.

- The Win Your Money Back Offer rocks because:

    o   You get loads of up front cash.

    o   You get more customers to say yes since you lower their risk.

    o   You get massive results for customers.

    o   You get more long-term customers.

    o   They advertise your offer to get you even more customers.

- Making some meetings a part of the terms gives great opportunities to check in with your customers and make more offers specific to their needs.

- Everyone thinks businesses make money on people who fail the program. No. The real money comes from people who succeed with it *and you have something else to offer them.* Trust me on this one. The more results you deliver, the more money you'll make. Think long.

- Make refund criteria easy to track, aligned with customer goals, and helpful for the business.

- Only use a Win Your Money Back Offer if your refund rate is below 5%. Otherwise, fix your product before doing this. You risk giving too many refunds.

- Put the store credit toward another, preferably more expensive, offer. You want them to stay customers…so give them the opportunity. You never want people to stop paying you.

- To make more sales and keep more customers, make everyone a winner in private. That way, everyone stays surprised and grateful when you make your Upsell Offer.

FREE GIFT: Win Your Money Back Offers Video Training

I've made a tremendous amount of money with this offer and I have more details and stories I couldn't reasonably fit in the book. If you want that, I made a free video for you, no opt-in required. To watch it, just go to acquisition.com/training/money. You can also scan the QR code if you hate typing.

Giveaways

Many will enter…many will win.

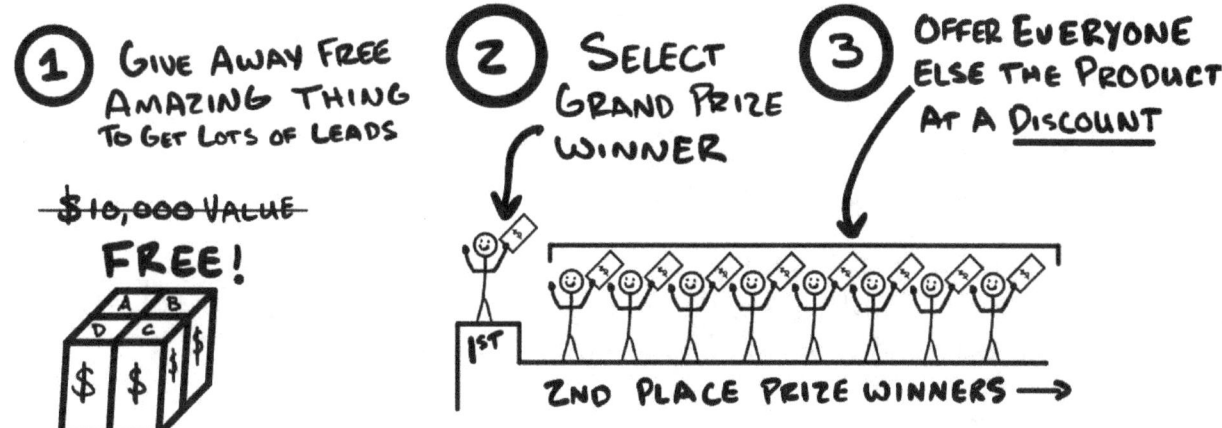

Disclaimer: Sweepstakes and giveaways are heavily regulated. Main reason: they're exceptionally powerful. And, when done wrong, can become illegal lotteries—we don't want that. Jail time—no bueno. Make sure you follow all the local advertising laws. This description is in no way a guarantee of lawfulness. I take no responsibility for anything you do or don't do as a result of reading this chapter. Whew—ok—got that outta the way.

August 2020.

I hopped on the phone with the owner of a fitness certification business to talk shop. In a few minutes, he gave me the rundown about how they certify fitness enthusiasts and help them find clients.

"Interesting business you've got," I said. "How do you get leads?"

"It's pretty simple. We advertise a full-ride scholarship to our entire program. People apply with their contact information and then answer a few questions. We ask stuff like 'Why should we pick you for the full-ride scholarship?' The best answer gets a full-ride. But we also do something more…"

"Nice, keep going…" I said.

"We give out partial scholarships."

"What do you mean? How does that work?"

"Well, we often have a clear winner for the full-ride. But tons of people have inspiring stories, so I want to make sure they got scholarships too. Now I can only give away one full-ride, but *I can give away as many partial scholarships as I want.*"

And then it hit me.

"Ooohhh… So lots of people apply for the 'grand prize' and only one person gets that. But the other applicants qualify for smaller prizes?"

"Right. So I make a big deal out of the person who wins the full-ride scholarship, but then I call everyone else to let them know they got a partial scholarship. When I talk to them, they're thrilled. Most of them join our program on the spot."

"So they don't know the actual price of your thing when they hop on the call?"

"Nope."

"But they know the *value* of the full-ride scholarship, and when you present the discounted price of your program with the partial scholarship, it's still huge savings."

"Exactly."

"So not only do you get tons of engaged leads, but you also get more customers with your 'surprise discount?' Genius."

"It works *really well*. We actually have to cap it to make sure we can service all the new sign-ups. Believe it or not, we teach the same play to the trainers we certify. It works just as well to get fitness customers—sometimes even better."

"Love it."

***

He presented this as an education offer and as a fitness offer. But it's so much more. I'm gonna show you how to use it in *any* business. Free Giveaways generate many leads who show interest in *your most expensive product.* What could be better?

Description

Giveaway Offers advertise a chance to win a big prize in exchange for contact information and whatever else you want. Then, after picking a winner, you offer everyone else the big prize at a discounted price. Giveaways also go by names like "scholarship" and "sweepstakes" and "raffles" etc. They all mean "enter for a chance to win." To run a Giveaway Offer you:

- Pick a Grand Prize.

- Pick your promotional offer.

- Ask for contact information and other eligibility criteria.

- Pick what actions you want entrants to take to qualify for the big prize.

- Put the giveaway on a deadline to add urgency.

- Announce the Grand Prize winner and contact everyone else.

Let's go into each with more detail.

Pick A Grand Prize. Make your Grand Prize *the thing you want everyone to buy.* Make sure you assign a monetary value to your grand prize to serve as a price anchor. For instance, if you sell $5,000 worth of value for $2,000, then advertise the $5,000 value!

Pick Your Promotional Offer. Your promotional offer takes the place of the "partial scholarship" in the story. You create it by enhancing your core offer with a discount, a bonus, or by minorly changing it from the Grand Prize in order to ethically justify a price reduction (using the Grand Prize as a price anchor). And the bigger the discount, the more compelling the offer. So the bigger the value you assign your Grand Prize, the better!

Remember, leads entered the Giveaway because they found the Grand Prize interesting. It gets you qualified leads because you offer what they already *showed interest in* at a discount. Call your promotional offer—the thing you sell to everyone else—whatever you want for your giveaway: scholarship, gift card, dollars off, store credit, vouchers, etc.

Ask For Contact Information. In exchange for a chance to win, ask for permission to contact them any way you please for follow-up promotions. Beyond that, I survey for prize *eligibility* and then ask them to take *qualifying actions.*

Eligibility. I ask if they're a fit for my products. Like *'Do you own a vet clinic?'* or more character/need-based questions like *'Why should you be selected?'*

Qualifying Actions. Other stuff entrants do to qualify to win. I also use these to get them to promote my giveaway more, or demonstrate higher levels of interest. Ex: attending a call or event, making a post, entering a group, etc.

Put The Giveaway On A Deadline To Add Urgency. Set a date for the Grand Prize drawing. Make your Giveaway more urgent by only making it available for a limited time. I like three to seven days from the day I start promoting it. As soon as leads enter the Giveaway—update them daily. First, let them know how long they have left until you announce the winner. You can do this with email, direct messages, texts, social media posts, and so on. Do as many as reasonable. Once a day across all platforms works fine. Second, provide value along with your countdown. Show everyone the benefits of the grand prize, how excited they should be, and *refer everyone to social proof.* Keep the hype alive!

Pro Tip: Whisper–Tease–Shout

Once people enter the Free Giveaway, it may help to think of the countdown like a mini-product launch. So check out the Affiliates and Partners chapter of *$100M Leads* for a detailed look on launches.

Announce The Grand Prize Winner And Start Contacting Everyone Else. Announce the Grand Prize winner publicly, then message everyone else who qualifies for your core offer <u>privately</u>. The beauty is—*everybody else qualifies for your promotional offer.* Notify them by text, email, and direct messages. In that message, ask them to schedule a call because they qualified for something else. If you need a reason—just say you found their answers/story so compelling you felt obligated to give them something just for entering. Think of your promotional offer like a "participation trophy."

To make sure they redeem, add another deadline. Make claiming your promotional offer (the scholarship, gift card, dollars off, store credit, vouchers, etc.) expire in seven days. The second countdown works like the first: show the benefits, more social proof, and more valuable stuff about your offer. Give them a way to book a call to claim the promotional offer.

Explain The Cost-To-Value *Using Their Discount.* My rule of thumb: make your core offer discount equal to 10%–30% of your gross margins. Say we advertise a Grand Prize with a $5,000 value with a $2,000 retail price tag. Everyone else gets it for $1,800 (a 10% discount off retail). When we let them know they qualified *for something*, we explain they get $5,000 in value for an $1,800 price tag. By comparing the value of the thing to what they pay, a 10% discount becomes a 64% difference in cost-to-value!

Bottom Line: Remember, everyone that entered the Giveaway showed interest in your thing. And if somebody shows interest in a thing you have to offer—*offer it to them.*

Example Free Giveaways

Dentist Offer—Free Perfect Smile Giveaway

Grand Prize: A free set of invisible braces—$6,000 retail price

Promotional Offer: $2,000 gift card for braces

Physical Products Offer—Free Year Of Organic Dog Food

Grand Prize: Free Year of Organic Dog Food—$1,000 retail price

Promotional Offer: $300 gift card for dog food *only useable with a one-year subscription*

Services Offer—Free Ultimate Giveaway

Grand Prize: Free 1-Year Package—$5,000 retail price

Promotional Offer: $2,000 voucher redeemable toward 1-Year Service Agreement

Consulting Offer—Free 16-Week Turnaround Giveaway

Grand Prize: 16-Week Turnaround—$12,000 retail price

Promotional Offer: $6,000 Partial Scholarship

Important Notes:

Consult Legal Counsel About How To Structure Your Giveaway. I'm not legal counsel, but I do consider these no-brainers because of the way I like to do business: somebody actually has to win the Grand Prize. Make the Grand Prize, and qualifications to win, clear in the rules. Make clear that more than one person can win a prize. Ask your legal counsel about the rest.

Eligibility Criteria Get More Customers To Buy Your Core Offer. More people will take your core offer if you can make the value *specific* to them. I ask questions like this to get ammo: Why should we pick you? Why this program? Why now? Why does this matter to you? Why is this important to you? What's your goal? Etc.

That being said, the more work you make it to enter the fewer people will enter, but the more qualified they'll be—*so find your sweet spot.*

If Your Giveaway Doesn't Work, It Means Your Grand Prize Wasn't Grand Enough.

One of my portfolio companies ran a giveaway. They barely got interest. Their grand prize? Tickets to their event. Not compelling. I told them *grand* prizes only work if they're grand. They tried it again with a $50,000 bundle of equipment from a well-known industry supplier *plus* their core product for a year. And, this time, it crushed (surprise).

When you have an awesome thing to give away *and* you advertise it properly, the leads flood in. And "Giveaway" kinda explains itself. So if nobody bites, then I suggest you give away something better. Or at least, better *for the audience.*

Give Away Two Prizes For Twice The Leads. If you give away one prize, that's fine. But if you give away <u>two</u> grand prizes, you can get twice the leads (or more). Here's how. Just tell everyone that if someone they refer wins the grand prize, they win one too. That way, they get endless 'entries' into the contest by referring their friends. This gets more people to refer (and work together). This also provides a sneaky benefit. Referrers are invested in the success of their referrals. This keeps quality high. Here's an example I did for Skool.com, a platform I co-own for people to build and monetize communities.

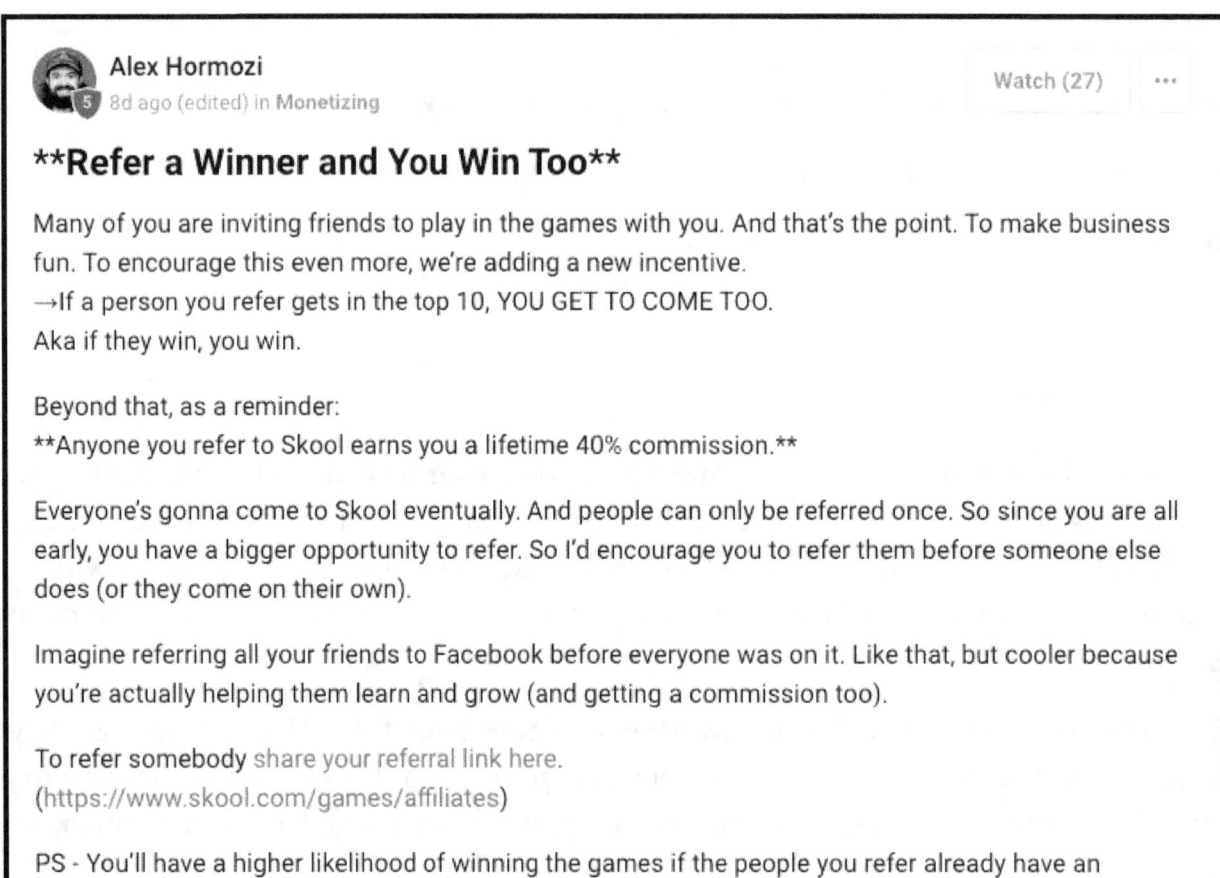

Scarcity, Scarcity, Scarcity. Limit your giveaway by time, number of entries, or both. You can run giveaways for a specific amount of time (ex: seven days), a specific number of entries (ex: 5,000 entries), or both. I like both. I match how many people I let enter the giveaway with the number of people I have the time and resources to connect with inside seven days. Any more would be a waste.

Urgency, Urgency, Urgency. I add urgency in three places—to enter, to claim, to use. Make how long they have to <u>enter</u> clear in the advertisements. Once you announce the winner(s), let them know how long they have to <u>claim</u>. When they do, schedule their call the same day or the next day (if you can). Once you let people know what they won, tell them how long they have to <u>use</u> it. I like hours, but I have gone up to five days. In short, *always have deadlines.*

Have Downsells Available. Some won't or can't buy your promotional offer, even with the discount or bonus. And that's okay. Here's how I approach it: at the start of the call, let them know they qualified for two prizes. And that you'll help them find which way makes the most sense for them. Then, present your promotional offer first—aka, the discount on the Grand Prize thing. If they take it, great. If not, then offer the same discount <u>by percentage</u> on any other product you have that makes sense for them.

If You Have A Recurring Revenue Business. Apply their discount over the longest period of time they'll agree to. Then, set up their monthly subscription to bill automatically at normal rates after the discounted period ends.

Summary Points

- At their core, Giveaways ask an audience to apply to get a high-value thing of yours for free. Many will enter—one wins. The rest qualify for discounts on your core offer.

- Pick a Grand Prize people want.

- Give two prizes away if you want more people to refer. Tell them if someone they refer wins, they win the other prize.

- Offer a chance to win the Grand Prize to anyone who enters *and* qualifies.

- You can get great information from every lead because you can make it part of the entry process. Get information that indicates how your offer will provide them value. This becomes important for making offers later.

- Advertise your Giveaway for seven days, or until the number of leads surpasses the number of people you can manage to call in seven days, whichever comes first.

- Book appointments with everyone else to claim your promotional offer. Use whatever "reason why" feels good to you.

- Putting an expiration date on people claiming their prize makes them more likely to claim it.

- If somebody says no to your core offer, have another product or service to discount. It may suit the lead better.

FREE GIFT: Giveaways Bonus Training

Giveaways are one of the strongest attraction offers on earth. They're so good they need to be regulated. I mean—who doesn't want somethin' for nothin', right? I made a free video training that covers the topic in depth. If you love this stuff as much as me, you can check it out at acquisition.com/training/money. As always, you can also scan the QR code if you hate typing. Enjoy.

Decoy Offer

Which one do you think will get you the best results?

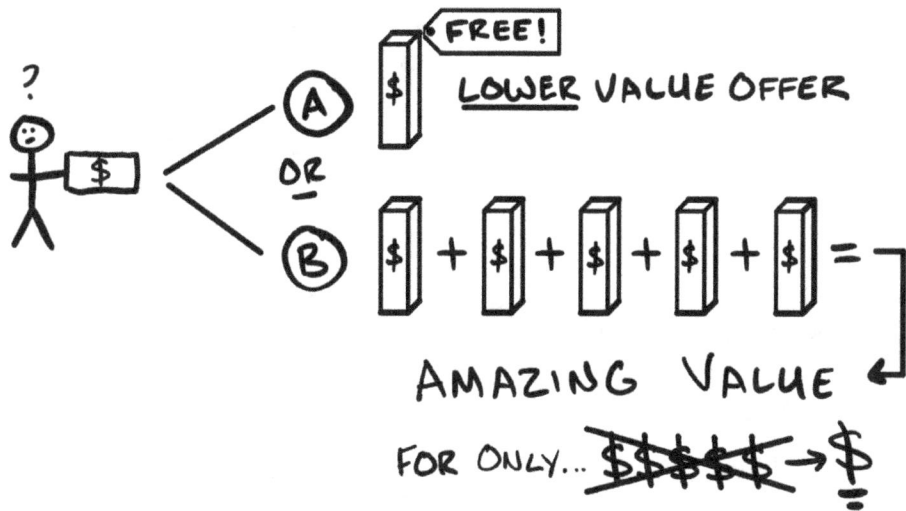

June 2014.

John, another early mentor, retired early. He spent his retirement raising his girls, playing golf, and hanging out at his lake house. He was a man who had lived.

Once in a while, he'd invite me to his lake house. And on those long drives, he taught me things about life and business that I use to this day. Like the difference between price and value. The pros and cons of low-cost offers. High-volume, low-price business models. Differences between recurring subscriptions and one-time transactions. And the art of keeping things *simple* in business and life.

John was great company. I often wished we could drive forever so I could soak everything in. To him, this was just another story to pass the time. But to me, it was a lesson I would never forget:

The 5-Day $5 VIP Tanning Pass.

"You see, the beauty of the 5-Day Pass is everyone thinks they can get tan in five days. And they can. But, it's never as tan as they want to get. And if they try to 'speed things up'... they'll burn. So, when someone comes in with a pass, we ask them how tan they wanna get. As soon as they say they want to get a few shades darker, we give them 'the turkey talk'."

"What's the turkey talk?" I asked.

John smiled and continued. "Say a Thanksgiving turkey takes three hours to cook. We all know what happens if you double the temperature to cook it in half the time—you burn it! It takes at least five to ten sessions to get the color they want *without burning*. And since they gotta take some time between sessions, it always takes more than five days. Once they realize that we say:

"'Let's just credit your VIP pass toward your first month. Why buy so many $25 day passes when members get unlimited access for just $19.99?'

"They immediately see the value and take the membership. Easy as that."

Five years later…

"Hey boss, we've got a problem."

Oh boy… "What's up?" I said.

"Our fitness leads have gotten way too expensive. The guys who can sell are still making it work, but most of them are barely breaking even."

"Dang, so it finally happened," I said. I pressed my hands to my forehead. I knew this was coming. And the truth is, I was dreading it.

I tried for weeks to put a "spin" on our previous offer. A new or interesting twist would buy us time, but our tests so far fell flat. *Crap.*

"You got any more offers up your sleeve?" he asked.

I racked my brain then remembered the $5 VIP Tanning pass. *That just might work.* "Why don't we offer something super cheap to get the leads, but when they come in, make them a crazy offer that costs more but is 100x better. They can still take the cheap thing, but we'll just explain that they'll get way better results with extra accountability, nutrition, etc."

"Yea, I can run something like that."

A few weeks later…

"Alex, I think we cracked it."

"Awesome! Walk me through it."

"So we give two options. The first option is free. I give one session per week. The second option is an 'Ultimate' Version for $399. It comes with unlimited sessions, 1–1 coaching, more personalized stuff, and a guarantee they'll get results or they repeat the program for free…"

"Oh man…that guarantee is *solid*. What's the take rate?"

"We got about eight out of ten people to take the $399 option. We're crushing it."

"Awesome—let's scale it!"

***

John was a brilliant salesman and patient teacher. His philosophy of *giving customers what they want now, so you can give them what they need later* shaped many ways I do business. He also inspired the offer that saved my gym. But the most valuable thing I learned from him was: "You have to know what gets results for customers better than they do. This makes our premium offer the clear solution." And making our premium the clear solution is what Decoy Offers are all about.

Description

Decoy Offers advertise something free or discounted. Then, when leads ask to learn more, you *also* present a more valuable premium offer. The premium offer provides more features, benefits, bonuses, guarantees, and so on. By putting your decoy offers and premium offers side-by-side, leads can see how much more valuable your premium offer is. I like Decoy Offers because they get more customers overall. They either take the decoy version or the premium version. If they take the premium, great. If they take the decoy, also great. It gives you time to upgrade them rather than losing them. But either way, you can close everyone. This makes it cheap and profitable to get new customers. And *any* business can use it.

Here are the steps to make a Decoy Offer:

1) Advertise a lesser, smaller, or simpler version of your premium offer as a decoy.

2) When leads engage, offer both options, but emphasize the premium one.

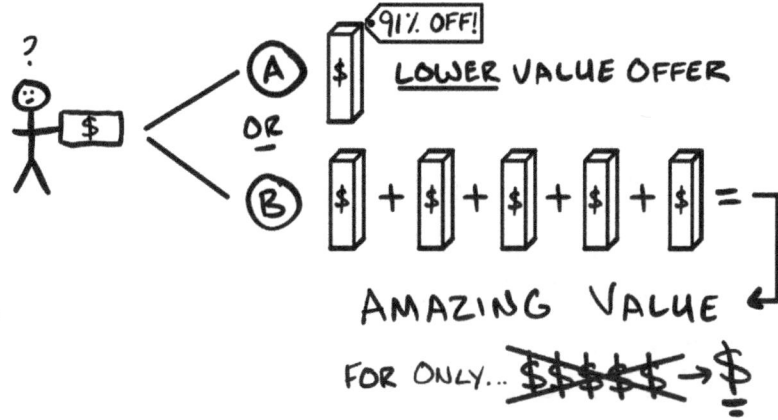

Examples

Lemonade Stand Offer (Physical Products)

Attraction Offer: "Free Week of Lemonade" **OR** "$1 Week of Lemonade."

Decoy Option: "You can have this water + powdered lemon + corn syrup" Or…

Premium Option: "The organic, all-natural, vegan, gluten-free, imported Italian lemons, which are cold-processed and shipped straight to your door. You'll never need to waste time coming to the store again. It'll have you feeling like a labrador puppy chasing butterflies all day. It also comes with other flavors, like our sparkling rosewater lemonade."

Float Tank Center (Service)

Attraction Offer: "Free 6-Week Stress Release" **OR** "$6 6-Week Stress Release."

Decoy Option: One float per month with at-home do it yourself stress relief exercises.

Premium Option: Two times per week floats for 6 weeks, 1–1 consulting, journal, sleep routine. Satisfaction guaranteed.

Gym Offer (Local Business)

Attraction Offer: "Free 21-Day Transformation" **OR** "$21 21-Day Transformation."

Decoy Option: Workouts done in a Skool.com group once a day. A general nutrition plan. Can watch recordings. No support. No guarantee.

Premium Option: Unlimited workouts, a personalized nutrition plan, 1–1 accountability, results guaranteed (or you get another 21 days free).

Important Notes

How To Make Your Decoy Offer. Offer fewer components, older models, or fewer personalized versions of your premium offer. Also, remove any guarantees. Your Attraction Offer only has to get leads to engage. Nothing more.

Advertise Benefits Not The Features. We want to sell them on the dream outcome. We advertise a *transformation* in 21 days, not workouts and meal plans. Leads get specific product details in the sales presentation, *not* in the advertising! Private jets and rowboats can both get you to an exotic island, but the premium option is certainly more enjoyable.

You Can Advertise Discounts in Four Ways. Let's say you had a year-long thing that costs $100 per month. If you wanted to let them pay $900 for the year, you could say:

1) Percentage Off: 25% off

2) Absolute Amount: $300 off

3) Free Portion: 3 Months Free

4) The Total Package: One Year For $900 (~~$1,200~~)

They all mean the same thing. It's worth testing to see which one converts better in your market.

Make The Contrast Huge. The value of the premium option comes from huge differences with the decoy option. So make the decoy option as basic as reasonable. Then make the premium option as awesome as possible. The bigger the contrast, *the better the deal*, and the more customers will take it.

Discount Offers Have Higher Show-Up Rates Than Free Offers. In my experience, If you run a Free Attraction offer, you'll get more leads. If you run a Discount Offer, you'll get fewer leads, but a higher percentage will show up. So if you have low show-up rates for appointments, try a Discount Offer instead. This is especially important for businesses where you have a high cost of someone not showing up (think doctors, lawyers, dentists, etc).

If Possible, Present The Premium Offer First. In a perfect world, they take the premium offer immediately. The decoy offer stays in your back pocket. If they come in specifically asking for the decoy option up front…

Get Them To Give You Permission To Sell Them. If they ask to hear about your decoy, you are legally required to present it, or you prefer to present it first, here's how I like to do it:

Ask them a simple question: *"Are you here for free stuff or lasting results?"*

And as soon as they say "results," which most people do, skip to your premium offer.

If they say "free stuff," present the decoy offer then immediately contrast it with your premium offer. Then only <u>after</u> presenting <u>both</u>, ask them *"which do you think will get you to your goal faster?"* or *"which would you prefer: XXX less valuable benefit or YYY more valuable benefit 1, 2, 3…?"* At this point, they'll have to say the premium offer. Then you can move forward in the sale mutually agreeing it's the best thing for them.

When Making Your Premium Offer, *Get Excited About It.* Present it as superior to the decoy offer, because it is. And, assuming it is, how it fits the customer better. Your excitement motivates people to take the options that will give them the most value.

From a selling perspective, you want to talk to the lead as if you already know they will accept your offer. Many salespeople refer to this as an "assumed close." You operate from a position of: *This is what everyone does. This is just a formality. Let me get your ID and credit card so you can get your value.* No hype. Just friendly disposition. Almost bored over how regularly people buy.

Surprise Benefit (Optional). To take this a step further, if someone takes the decoy option, you can choose to surprise them with a few low-/zero-cost features from your premium offer. Just say something like "hey, I'm gonna throw this in, even though it's part of our premium offer just because I want you to get great results." This builds goodwill, over delivers, and increases the chance they take your upsells later. Remember—they're still leads!

Summary Points

- Decoy Offers advertise something free or discounted. Then, when leads ask to learn more, you *also* present a more valuable premium offer.

- Make the premium option *far* more valuable than the decoy option by adding more features, benefits, bonuses, and guarantees.

- Strip down your Decoy Offer as much as reasonable.

- When leads ask about your Decoy Offer, present your premium offer right next to it.

- Ask *"are you here for free stuff or lasting results?"* for permission to offer the premium thing first.

- You can still make money from leads who pick the decoy option. You'll learn the best way to deliver your decoy product *and* maximize upsells from it.

- Expect to make money fast. If you're not, then make the contrast between offers larger.

FREE GIFT [No Opt-in Required]: Decoy Offers Training

Decoy Offers are one of the most flexible attraction offers. You just need to know more about your customer's problem than they do. They're also easy to train people to sell. I've run them in a number of different industries. If you want to nerd out on the topic, I made a full video breakdown for you. You can check it out at acquisition.com/training/money. As always, you can also scan the QR code if you hate typing.

Buy X Get Y Free

Buy one puppy, get two puppies free!

BUY X GET Y FREE

PRODUCTS:

BUY 1 SHIRT   GET 2 FREE!

$20   FREE!   FREE!

SERVICES:

 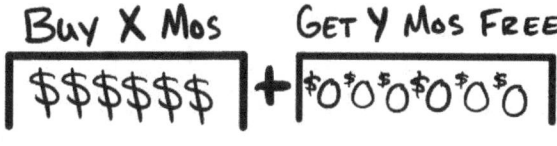

BUY X MOS   GET Y MOS FREE

Downtown Nashville 2020.

Bars and shops at this popular tourist destination went in and out of business all the time, but one store reigned supreme: *Boot Factory.* Their neon sign cut through the visual clutter on the street like a hot knife through butter. A cowboy boot bigger than my car—directing me to the front door. There was no mistaking what they wanted me to do. So of course, I obeyed. And as I got closer, I could make out their offer:

BUY 1 PAIR GET TWO PAIR FREE

A decade passed since I'd been to Nashville. But, I remembered the sign and the buy-one-get-two-free offer like it was yesterday. As a kid on bar crawls, I thought the offer was dumb. "How could they give away so much stuff and stay in business?" But now, with some offer-making under my belt, I could appreciate it.

I went straight to the men's section and grabbed a boot. Curious, the price was marked down *twice*—to a "final offer" of $600 for the pair. But these were normal-looking boots? The young me would've scoffed. But business me realized I had missed something. The store got much bigger since the last time I saw it, so the offer clearly worked. Then it clicked.

They charged three times the price for a single pair of boots because they came with two more pairs. So rather than saying "come to *Boot Factory* and buy boots at a fair price" they managed to create a free offer! Even in the few minutes I checked out the store, bachelorettes filed in to get matching boots. And since the *Boot Factory* sat in the middle of a street full of cowboy-themed bars, this happened a lot. It was *brilliant*.

Description

In Buy X Get Y Free Offers, when customers buy something, they get other stuff free. The more free stuff they get, and the higher its value, the better it works. Free offers get *way* more attention than Discount Offers. But if you only have one thing to sell, and you give it away, *you go hungry.* In situations like this, businesses tend to lean on discounts. They run "sales" relying on holidays, seasonal changes, or whatever, as reasons to *temporarily* lower prices and get more customers.

But, by selling more than one thing at once, you can turn Discount Offers into even stronger *Free Offers.* When you have more than one item, you can make the discount value large enough that it covers the price of more stuff. For example, I could sell three t-shirts for $10 each for a total of $30 *or* I could sell one t-shirt for $30 and give two away free. It's the same price, but *way more free stuff!*

And if I wanted to offer a discount (rather than *only* reframe the price) I could do this. I could sell three t-shirts for $6.67 each for a total of $20 (33% discount) *or* keeping the same discount, I could sell one t-shirt for $20 and give two away free. It's the same price, but *way more free stuff again!*

Boot Factory took the first option. They tripled the price of one pair of boots and added value…in more boots. And an expensive pair of boots with two free pairs gets *Boot Factory* more customers than selling one pair at a fair price. Plus, if you can include *free* then it attracts even more customers.

Examples

Buy 1 Get 2 Free Physical Products Offer: (The *Boot Factory* Offer)

- One Pair of Boots: $200

- Buy X Get Y Free Offer: Buy One Pair For $600, Get Two Pairs for Free

- End Result: They still buy three pairs of $200 boots for a total of $600

3 Versions: 18 Months Of Services AKA "3 Pairs Of Boots"

- Good: *"Buy 12 Months Get 6 Months Free"* - $1,800

- Better: *"Buy 9 Months Get 9 Months Free"* - $1,800

- Best: *"Buy 6 Months Get 12 Months Free"* - $1,800

Everyone pays the same price for the same amount of service. But, the third option is the most compelling. (Hint: It has the most free stuff!)

Important Notes

Buy X Get Y Free Gets People To Buy More Stuff *And* Provides More Value. It used to take a whole year for some of my service businesses to make their money. But the "Buy 6 Months Get 6 Months Free" offer attracted *far* more customers than the original month-to-month offer. Even better, they got paid up front for it!

Raise Prices Before Giving Stuff Away To Preserve Profits. If you use this to attract customers, it will work. And since it will work, you need to make money. So, *permanently* raise prices to accommodate the discount. Don't lie. Actually raise your prices. Since this is what all new customers will be coming in on, then it makes sense to change it, for a season at least. Plus, plenty of people might still take your doubled prices a la carte and break your limiting beliefs around pricing. You're welcome.

Buy X Get Y Free Works Better If You Have More Free Stuff Than Paid Stuff.

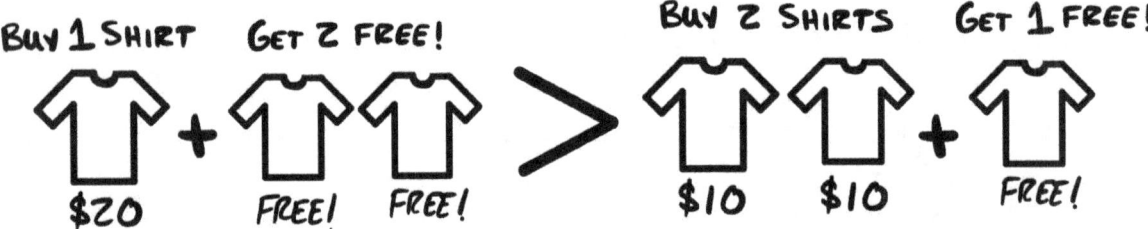

See second example. Buy ten get two free is not as strong as buy two get ten free. This seems obvious, but again, people don't do it. To make it work better, give more free than you ask people to buy. Just play with the pricing until it makes sense for you. 'Buy one get two' instead of 'buy two get one'.

The Free Things Can Be Different From The Paid Things.

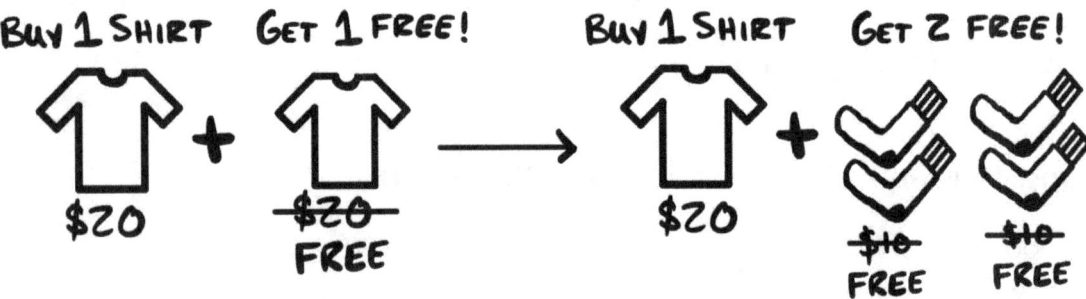

When people first start doing offers like this, they match the free and paid stuff. But you can mix and match whatever you want. Just make sure the value of the *different* free stuff still makes the offer compelling. Ex: Let's say socks have a $10 value. If they buy one shirt for $20 but get $20 of free socks, it may seem like a better deal.

More Free Cheaper Things Can Work Better Than Fewer Free Expensive Things.

Revisiting the t-shirt example. Let's say I could only afford to give one shirt away for free, but for the same cost I could give them three pairs of socks. I'd probably test "Buy 1 Shirt Get 1 Shirt Free" against "Buy 1 Shirt, Get _3_ Socks Free." Socks cost less than a shirt but people still see "buy <u>one</u> thing get <u>three</u> things free." Sometimes, *more* cheaper things work better than *fewer* expensive things.

Rather Than Offer a 33% Discount, Try Buy One Get Two Free.

Even though it can be structured to accomplish the same thing, free drives more interest than a discount. More people know the value of *free* than the value of one shirt. For example, rather than sell $10 shirts for $6.67 each (33% off), you may get more interest (and make more money) by offering "buy one shirt for $20 get two free." Test it.

Do Not Make Offers Like This If You Can't Manage Money. While Buy X Get Y Free offers create massive cash flow for a business, you need to deliver. So if you get a whole year's worth of payments in a month, *make sure you can deliver* for the whole year. Budget the correct amount of money to service your customers for the duration of your agreement. Don't be a goon and buy yourself a house with the cash meant for servicing your customers. Selling stuff you can't deliver on breaks the law and *ruins* your reputation. Deliver on your promises.

Make This Offer To Existing Customers For Fast Cash. If you have a recurring business already, and need cash fast, you can make this offer to existing customers. Many will happily 'Buy Ten and Get Two Free' even at their current price. Just limit the offer to 10% of your customers. This gives you a good cash pop *and* keeps recurring cash flow healthy.

Don't Worry. Prepaid Customers Keep Buying Stuff. So, Keep Selling It To Them. A lot of people don't want to make more offers to customers who prepay for stuff. This is a mistake. Speaking from experience, these are people who spend the most money. Give them other offers to buy, and they will. After all, they may have prepaid months ago. Their wallets have been 'refreshed' with new money that is dying to make it into your pocket. Don't get in the way!

If Customers Only Buy Once, Make Them Buy Big. The *Boot Factory* in my story catered to tourists that want to fit in the local cowboy bars. This means most of their customers made *one* purchase. Ever. For that reason, it makes sense to make that purchase as large as possible. Just provide the value to back it up. If you only have one shot, you may as well make it count!

Summary Points

- In Buy X Get Y Free Offers, when customers buy something, they get other stuff free.

- Buy X Get Y Free works for stuff that makes sense to buy more of or get longer access to.

- Basic Buy X Get Y Free offers reframe pricing. Buy 1 Get 2 Free costs the same as buying 3…except customers see the free offer as more valuable. (18 Months of Service example)

- Always try to give more free things than paid things.

- You can pair different free things with your paid things.

- Some Buy X Get Y Free offers discount the price—where buying more things costs less per thing than buying the same number of things one at a time.

- Buy X Get Y Free can lengthen the amount of time customers stay. If normal customers stay for three months, then 'Buy 2 Get 2 Free' will keep them for four months (or whatever you set it at). This gives you more opportunities to make more offers and provide more value.

- If you use Buy X Get Y Free to generate a lot of cash fast, make sure you manage it well and deliver on your promises.

- If you need fast cash, you can make this offer to existing recurring customers. Just cap how many you sell so you still have cash flow.

- Keep selling customers who prepay long durations, they are the most likely customers to buy again!

FREE GIFT: Buy X Get Y Free Video Course

Buy X Get Y Free get lots of cash and lots of customers. You just need to know your math. I made a free video for you giving a few more creative ways to use it. You can watch the video fo' free at acquisition.com/training/money. Scan the QR code if you hate typing.

Pay Less Now or Pay More Later

Time is money. - Benjamin Franklin

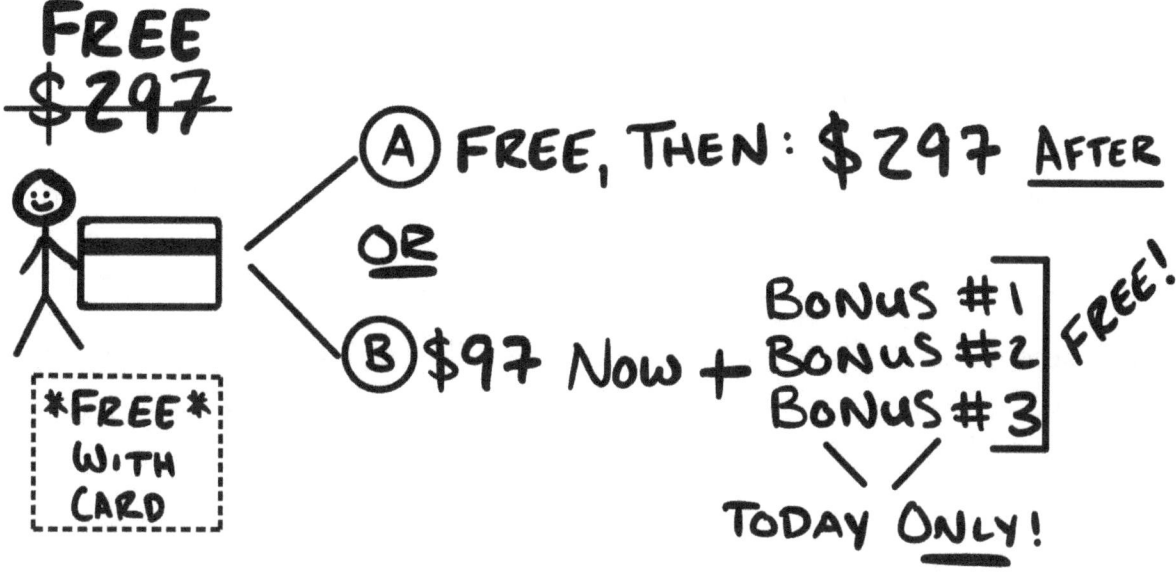

June 2016.

A headline caught my attention: *"Double your reading speed in 3 hours, or it's free."* I opened and scanned the text. Inside, the world's fastest reader offered a free training to double my reading speed in three hours. So, I registered. Why not?

The registration page said, "You can put your credit card down for $0, and get billed $297 tomorrow. And if your reading speed doesn't double, just email us before then and we'll cancel the charge. But you must attend in order to be eligible." *or* "You can just pay $97 right now, and as a free bonus, get the recordings, which won't be for sale anywhere else."

I decided on the first option. I wanted to see if my reading speed doubled before paying for anything. The whole training I expected him to sell me more stuff. But he simply provided value. After two hours, using his tactics, my reading speed doubled. *Impressive.* The training had been true to the promise. He earned his $297.

After that, he talked about how I could learn to read even faster with his eight-week training program. I was satisfied with my results, so I chose not to take the upsell. He taught me a skill I still use to this day. But, the true value came from learning a brand new Attraction Offer.

Description

In Pay Less Now or Pay More Later, you give people a choice to pay full-price later OR pay a discounted price now. This play works so well because we remove *all* risk from the customer. They pay later *and* only if they like it. So it combines the benefits of a delayed payment and a satisfaction guarantee. *Anyone can sell this.* Almost anyone will agree to pay later if they are satisfied. But, once they agree to pay later, you can get them to pay *now* with hefty discounts and valuable bonuses.

The *pay later* option allows you to advertise "free" since they can choose to pay or not. This gets lots of leads engaged. But this free offer has an added benefit—*we get their card on file*. If they choose this option and hate the product, then they can cancel any time before the charge goes through.

If they accept the *pay later* option, we make a follow up offer to *pay now. Pay now* options provide a 20–50% discount and greater bonuses. And since we already have their card on file, we make it easy for them to pay.

Whether they choose to *pay now* or *pay later*, you've got customers, and likely, some profit. But, to take full advantage of this offer, you'll want something else to sell. So have something *more, better, newer* to offer when the time is right. And don't worry, we go deep on upsells in the next section.

Examples

Find Your First Real Estate Deal—Free 3-Day Workshop

Pay Later: $0 for 3-day workshop. They get billed $500 at the end unless they cancel.

Pay Now: $299 for 3-day workshop plus recordings, 1–1 call with certified distressed property expert, plus printed materials to use (delivered at the workshop).

Upsell: $30,000 to take you through every other step of closing your first deal within six months *plus*: legal templates, advisor to vet the investment, inspection checklist, etc.

Local Business Service: Trim Your Hedges For Free

Pay Later: $0 Lawn Cut + Hedges then $599 after.

Pay Now: $369 Lawn Cut + Hedges + Lawn Treatment.

Upsell: $199 per month lawncare services.

The rep comes to the house, makes the estimate, and offers both options, then upsells after the work is done.

Physical Products: 14-Day Clothing Trial

Pay Later*: $0 Now. Get it. Then get billed $149 in 14 days.

Pay Now: $97 for the clothing + an accessory that goes with it.

Upsell: The dress comes with an offer for a monthly subscription to more clothes like this.

Customers must return the product in like-new condition before billing to qualify for guarantee.

Important Notes

Promise A Clear Yes/No Result. First, make your promise a clear 'yes or no' result. Second, make sure you can deliver on it within your time frame. If you don't, they will ask not to be billed. Duh. For example, if you promise to decrease someone's shoulder pain, have them rate their pain 1–10 before you do your magic, then ask them to rate it after. If it went down, you've succeeded and you can sell them something else. Keep the promise simple, clear, and measurable. This avoids unnecessary cancellations.

Make a <u>Conditional</u> Satisfaction Guarantee. *People can only cancel the billing if they qualify.* For example, I had to show up to the reading training to qualify to cancel the charge. After all, they can't say you suck if they never try it. So, be sure to track the conditions necessary to qualify. Think: attendance, showing up to an appointment, turning in data, etc. Make the criteria what people do to get the most value out of the product. Win-Win.

Bonuses For Your 'Pay Now' Option. I hate when people repeat content and call it new. So I didn't want to be like that. I dedicated an entire chapter to bonuses in my offers book: *$100M Offers*. You can grab a copy of the book, or watch the video training on my site for free at: acquisition.com/training/offers.

Optimizing Your 'Pay Now' And 'Pay Later' Offer. If too many people take your 'pay later' option, discount the 'pay now' option more, add better bonuses, or both. If too many people take your 'pay now' option, do the opposite.

If More Than 10% Of 'Pay Later' People Cancel Their Payment. You promised too much, the guarantee conditions are too low, or the price is too high. <u>Note</u>: No matter how well you deliver, *some* people will cancel their payment. That's okay. Factor it in your costs of doing business and live your life.

This Works For Recurring Revenue Businesses Too. You just give them the option to pay a higher ongoing rate 30 days later *or* they pay less today and keep the lower rate for good. Plus, add in some bonuses.

If You Run Events/Workshops/Presentations, Hint At Your Next Offer Early.

If the reading guru had said *"Everyone wants to know when my next reading intensive starts because they sell out so fast. I'll get to it at the end. But please pay attention. I want to deliver on the promise I made to you guys to double your reading speed first."* By hinting about his next offer earlier, he would've sold more of it. Let me explain:

I used to do *a lot* of nutrition consultations. People would interrupt me all the time to ask about supplements. It annoyed me. So one tired day I spouted *"everyone wants to know what supplements to buy. We'll get there—I promise. But please pay attention to the nutrition section—it matters more."* By accident, I implied everyone bought supplements *without offering them*. And all the head nods I got showed they actually did want more products. All these factors got more people to buy when they finally got to ask. A happy mistake I made sure to repeat.

Summary Points

- Pay Less Now Or Pay More Later Offers give people a choice to pay full-price later OR pay a discounted price *with* additional bonuses…*if they pay now.*

- The *Pay Later* option has a delayed payment with a conditional guarantee.

  o Have clear criteria to qualify for the guarantee and easy ways to measure it.

  o If you can, align the criteria with what gets people the most value from the product.

- The *Pay Now* option offers a 20–50% discount and bonuses *if they pay now.*

  o Offer customers the *pay now* option <u>after</u> they accept the *pay later* option.

  o If they choose *pay now,* they get the discount and bonuses *instead of* the guarantee.

- Make your promise easy to track, difficult to refute, and a clear yes/no result.

- If you have more than 10% canceling, you promised too much, the guarantee conditions are too low, or the price is too high.

  o Also, give extra attention to those who claim they haven't received what was promised before the cancellation deadline.

FREE GIFT: Pay Less Now Pay More Later Training [No Opt-in]

This is one of the most creative offers I've ever seen or used. It does exceptionally well with digital products and short duration services. These can be scary effective and also 'feel good.' It's super easy to teach salesmen as well. If you want to learn more about them I made a deeper training for you free at acquisition. com/training/money. Scan the QR code for easy fast access.

Free Goodwill Offer

He who said money can't buy happiness hasn't given enough away.

"I became a quadriplegic in 2018 and was living on welfare until I found your content and book…I made $50,000 the following 12 months as a freelancer." - Danny W.

I have a question for you…

<u>Would you help someone you've never met if it cost you nothing, but you didn't get credit?</u>

Most people do, in fact, judge a book by its cover. So here's my ask on behalf of a struggling entrepreneur you've never met: **Please help that entrepreneur by leaving this book a review. Your review helps…**

…one more small business like Bill's provide for their community. In Bill's own words: *"I opened a pizzeria in early 2022 shortly after finding $100M Offers. Sales started slow, but we did it! After I read $100M Leads we implemented many things like having customers donate to the local foodbank for a chance to win free pizza for a year. I've lost count of how many new customers we've gotten after doing these things for the community. This absolutely proves this stuff works for any type of business. Thank you!"*

…one more entrepreneur like Thomas support their family. In Thomas's own words: *"After ten years, I got laid off my 9–5 job. But then I found your book and opened a tour guide business in Colorado. Fast forward two years and we have 5 employees! I literally took what I learned and built my dream. Now my kids and wife are happier than ever."*

…one more employee like Miguel's have more meaningful work. In Miguel's own words: *"I received the book as a gift and decided to pass it on to my six employees. Since then, our business has undergone a remarkable transformation and continues to grow on a monthly basis. Not only that, but I also gave it to my independent contractor trainers. Thank you."*

Your review helps…one more entrepreneur like Simon transform their life. In Simon's own words: *"I'm just a normal guy from Germany and I couldn't get a client to save my life. Then I bought $100M Leads. After reading the Cold Outreach chapter I started the Rule of 100. I expected to mayyybe get 1-2 clients…But then…I booked 8 meetings in 7 days…I closed 4 of them and earned my first 500€ from one of the clients. It has been 3 months now and my career couldn't be better. Your book was the only book I needed. I recommend it to everybody!!"*

…one more entrepreneur like Alex get out of a hole. In Alex's own words: *"I moved in with my girlfriend making less than $1,000 per month. I bought $100M Leads and we applied EVERYTHING. 3 weeks later we signed a client for over $2,000 a month. Then, three more! I owe you A LOT more than what those books cost."*

Your review helps…one more entrepreneur like Mohan flee his country and get out of debt. In Mohan's own words: *"As a struggling Indian immigrant trying to get to Ireland. I made so little money I would die before I paid off my debt. I tutored on the side where I could. Then I read the $100M Offers and quit my job 11 days later. I did the same work but learned how to make offers this time. Clients were happy to pay. Sometimes even €1500 when I give some bonuses. I make a livable income now. And finally found what I love to do. I moved to Germany now and my debt is almost paid. Thank you, Alex."*

If you tell yourself you'll do it later, instead, please do it now. It takes less than 60 seconds to change someone's life forever.

If you are on Audible—hit the three dots in the top right of your device, click rate & review, then leave a few sentences about the book with a star rating.

If you are reading on Kindle or an e-reader—scroll to the bottom of the book, then swipe up and it will prompt a review for you.

If for some reason these changed—you can go to Amazon (or wherever you purchased this) and leave a review right on the book's page.

If you feel good about helping a faceless entrepreneur, you are my kind of people. Welcome to #mozination. You're one of us.

I'm that much more excited to help you make more money than you can possibly imagine. You'll love the tactics I'm about to share in the coming chapters. Thank you from the bottom of my heart. Now, back to our regularly scheduled programming.

- Your biggest fan, Alex

Attraction Offers Conclusion

Extra! Extra! Hear All About It!

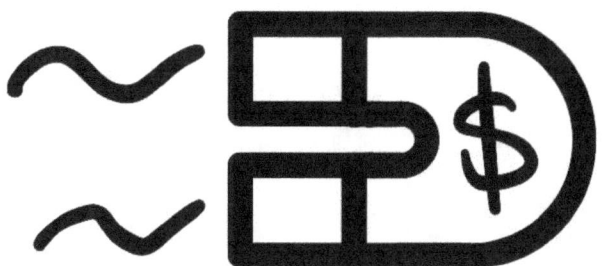

The point of Attraction Offers is to turn strangers into customers. And, to do it in a way that gets more cash up front. Ideally, we get enough cash to cover the cost of the customer and the cost to deliver our thing *multiple times over.* That way we can pay ourselves back *and* get our next customer.

I showed you the five most powerful Attraction Offers I've seen and used: Win Your Money Back, Giveaways, Decoy Offers, Buy X Get Y Free, and Pay Less Now or Pay More Later. I apply them at one time or another to every business I own. They turned $1,000 into $10,000,000 in ten months because when I got returns *I kept doubling down.* A Grand Slam Attraction Offer changes your business (and life) *forever.*

After using Attraction Offers, we've got more customers. And now that we got 'em, we need to boost our 30-day profits by selling them more stuff. This leads us to the next component of a *$100M Money Model*—Upsell Offers: *What to offer next.*

SECTION III: UPSELL OFFERS

Do you want fries with that? - McDonald's Famous Upsell

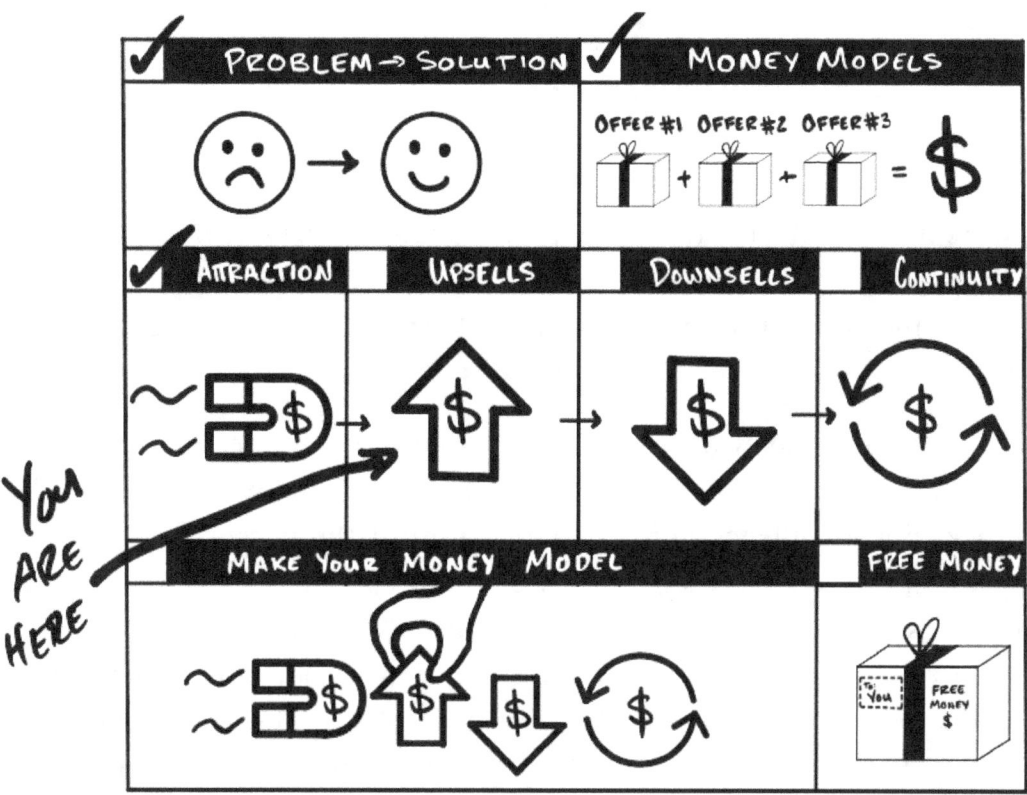

With an Attraction Offer in place, you've got customers and cash. If we did a good job, we've turned a profit too. Nice! Now we want to maximize 30-day profits. So what do we do? Answer: make more money. To do that, we make Upsell Offers. And when it comes down to it, Upsells just mean *whatever we offer next.*

How Upsells Work

UPSELLS

When an offer solves a problem, another appears. You *upsell* the solution to the problem your offer reveals. So, every offer opens the door to an upsell…even upsells! Often, upsells make the majority of the profit. They make or break a Money Model. Let me show you how much.

Let's say a burger shop makes $0.25 in profit on a $2.00 burger. If it was the only offer they had, they'd have to sell ~10,000 burgers a day to cover costs and *barely* eek out a "living." Good luck. But, they have more offers beyond just the burger. They ask *"Do you want fries with that?"* If they say yes, they profit another $0.75 and ask *"Do you want to make it a meal?"* which adds a drink. If someone says yes, they profit an *extra* $1.75. Their profit goes from $0.25 to $2.00—*an 8x increase*. And on top of that, they offer a third upsell *"Do you want to supersize your meal for just a buck more?"* This takes profit from measly $0.25 to a massive $3.00—*a 11.6x increase*. And now this little burger place actually has a chance at succeeding.

BURGER, FRIES $ SODA METHOD

PRICE: $2.00
COST: $1.75
PROFIT: .25

PRICE: $2.00
COST: $1.75
PROFIT: .25

+

UPSELL PRICE: $2.00
UPSELL COST: $.25
NEW PROFIT: $1.75

+

UPSELL PRICE: $1.00
UPSELL COST: $.10
NEW PROFIT: .90

MEDIUM

LARGE

OLD WAY

NEW WAY

8x GROSS PROFIT/SALE

11.6x GROSS PROFIT/SALE

I show this basic (and common!) example to point out one thing—your first offer *doesn't always* make the profit. In other words, *the thing you sell the most isn't always the thing you make the most profit on.* You make it on the second, third, and in the case of the burger business, fourth offers and beyond. If McDonald's didn't upsell fries and soda, there wouldn't be a McDonald's. If you want to win, you have to figure out your version of *"Do you want fries with that?"* If you don't, others will.

Upsells fail when:

- You offer something they don't want (too different or doesn't solve their problem).

- You offer it at the wrong time (before they've experienced the problem).

- You offer it the wrong way (they don't believe you).

- Or, a combination of the above.

In summary, Upsells tend to offer:

- *More* of what they just got (think quantity)—*Why have one burger when you can have two?*

- *Better* versions of it (think quality)—*Why have mystery meat when you can have sirloin?*

- *New* or complementary stuff (think different)—*Do you want fries and a soda with that burger?*

I Use Four Simple And Brutally Effective Upsell Offers:

- The Classic Upsell

- Menu Upsells

- Anchor Upsells

- Rollover Upsells

And with just a few tweaks, you can fit them into your business today. **Warning**: This section is brutally effective and must be used ethically. That being said, let's make some money.

FREE GIFT: Upsell Offers [No Opt-in]

If you want to make more profit per customer, you gotta sell them more stuff. Knowing the right time, way, and stuff to sell is key. I've learned my fair share of lessons doing it the wrong way. I hope I can help you avoid those mistakes and get it right the first time. I made you an additional training on this chapter you can watch for free at acquisition.com/training/money. QR code for easy fast access.

The Classic Upsell

You Can't Have X Without Y!

Summer 2016.

He was a premier fur coat dealer, a fourth-generation business savant, and a childhood mentor of mine. We sat down to catch up in a swanky restaurant across from his shop. Within a minute of ordering, our salmon appeared.

"What do you think this salmon costs the restaurant? Three bucks? Maybe a few extra pennies for the garnish? And look at the menu—they're charging thirty-two bucks! Unbelievable…but…we pay it." He took his first bite, chuckled to himself, then continued.

"So I heard you got into the game—good for you. Never would've guessed when you worked at the shop. You were kinda awkward."

"What can I say? Brushing seven thousand fur coats in a row melted my brain." I chuckled, "You still making a killing on that?"

A sheepish grin appeared. "Yeah. And that's not even the best part, my son came up with something genius." His son would be the *fifth-generation owner.*

"Tell me about it." I asked.

"We advertise free earmuffs with coat storage. And get this. When customers come to get their muffs and store their coats he says, *'Great. And we'll store those as well for $30. You don't want to store anything else do you?'* And of course, they say no."

"Wait a second, so you get them to pay for additional storage for the free ear muffs by getting them to say no? You guys are legends."

"Oh us? Noooo. We just stay creative…and if something works, we stick with it."

***

Whenever he talked business, he'd light up. Despite being awkward around his shop, I learned many lifelong lessons from him. I share this story in homage to those lessons.

Description

The Classic Upsell offers a solution to the customer's next problem *the moment* they become aware of it. I explain the Classic Upsell first because it's extremely profitable, easy, and anyone can do it. Main reason: current customers *always* have a higher chance of buying your stuff than strangers. And, when timed right, customers upsell themselves.

The Classic Upsell relies on knowing more about your customer's problem than they do. And you darn well should—it's your business after all. The idea is simple—your core offer solves one problem and creates another. *Your upsell immediately solves that next problem.* This gives the classic upsell its "You can't have X without Y" structure. Like the rental car story. You can't have a car without insurance. You can't have a car without gas. You can't have a good trip without a late checkout. Etc. And all of these things become immediately apparent *as soon as* the customer makes the first purchase.

Bottom Line: If a problem appears, and you can solve it immediately—in exchange for money—*do it!*

Examples

Local Car Wash Service

First purchase: Car Wash

Upsell: Sealant

You're not gonna wanna do the wash without sealant. You get way more for your money.

Physical Product

First Purchase: Bicycle

Upsell #1: Helmet

Upsell #2: Lights

Upsell #3: Puncture-Resistant Tires

You can't have a bike without a helmet!

Digital Product

First purchase: Course on exercising

Upsell: Nutrition course

You can't out-exercise a bad diet…so you're gonna want our course on nutrition.

Important Notes

Actually Do It. You'd be amazed how many businesses come to me and only sell one thing. I usually just tell them "You barely have a business—you have a front end. Figure out what you're gonna offer *next*." Months later, I hear they *actually* 5x'd their business because they *actually* offered an upsell.

Offer More Profitable Upsells First. If I offer two products and one has a higher profit than the other, I offer the higher profit option first.

Get Them To "Say No To Say Yes." I was always amazed at how often the fur coat dealer got people to buy stuff by saying "no." He knew people had been trained to say "no" in response to "you don't want anything else do you?" But this actually turns a "no" into "yes." So when upselling, the question translates to: *You don't want anything [besides what I just offered] do you?* Clever salesmanship. So let the nos (*yeses*) roll in.

Surprise And Delight. Let's say you have four bonuses you save to add to get people who are on the fence to buy. Add one at a time. If they say yes before you add them, still give them all four. It will surprise and delight them. And, it guarantees you still sell the same thing to everyone so no one feels left out later.

Sell More When They're Buying More—Hyper Buying Cycle. Most buyers enter a "hyper buying" cycle when they decide to do something new. It's a short window of time when they are the most excited about a new thing they're gonna do. This is when they spend a huge chunk of money in a short period of time. Think weddings, starting new hobbies, having babies, moving to new places, and so on. If you have a business that caters to these sorts of problems, don't shy away from Upsell Offers. *Embrace it...and keep making offers.*

Use Free Bonuses To Create Problems Upsell Offers Solve. Bonuses solve problems. That's what makes them valuable. And because of the problem-solution cycle, they can also reveal them. Upsells can solve that new problem. The ear muffs, for example, cost materials and labor. But they were able to 'give them for free' by getting customers to pay $30 to store something *they just got for free.*

The Faster People Get Access To Stuff, The More They'll Value It. A $10,000 thing you get later is worth less than a $10,000 thing you get now. The longer it takes someone to access something, the less value it has in the moment. So if you want to raise the chance of them taking the upsell, make it available as soon as you can. Bonus points if you put it in their hands before they've said yes. It's way harder to give something back than it is to say no.

If You Bundle Upsells, Name Them. It's easier to sell someone one thing than nine things. By bundling items together, you can make one 'ask' and get nine sales. I name the packages based on customer type *and/or* result. For example, "Fastest results" bundle or "Transformation package" or "Minimum package." All of these will boost upsells-per-person. Last, you can "peel" some of the products or features out of the package as a way to downsell. More on that in Section IV: Downsell Offers.

Integrate Upsells Into Your Other Offers. Make stuff you upsell part of how you deliver other offers. Then, more customers will take them. My meal plans included optional supplement suggestions. So when I went over nutrition, people asked about supplements. Gym Launch sales and marketing training suggested optional softwares. This led gym owners to buy them. Integrate the next thing you wanna sell into the first thing they buy.

Make Sure You Book-A-Meeting-From-A-Meeting (BAMFAM). The more times you can upsell, the more people you will upsell. If you upsell more people, you make more money. Since you want that...end every appointment by scheduling the next appointment. Don't let them leave without booking! As my big fancy public CEO friend Sharran says: "A customer should know the next time they see you—and why—*before they leave.*" So if you agree to meet again, *agree on why and when right then.*

Upsell As Many Times As It Makes Sense To. The rental car agency had lots of upsells. The burger place had lots of upsells. My gyms had lots of upsells. Gym Launch had lots of upsells. Offer as many solutions as there are problems you can solve. Don't be shy. If you can solve it, offer to. The second worst thing that happens is they say no. *The worst thing is if they would've said yes but you never asked.*

How To Upsell *More Of The Same Thing*

So if you have two things and want to sell one, add a third option to nudge the option you want them to buy. Movie theaters do this with soda and popcorn. Here's how:

Their Small - Medium - Large pricing works something like this:

A - Small - $5

B - Medium - $8 *(Rather than the rational price of $7)*

C - Large - $9

Result: More people take large. People who will take the small option will always take the small option. People who take the large will always take the large. *But the people who normally take medium will now probably take the large.*

If you want to get more people to buy the *medium* option, you'd price it like this:

Small - $6 *(Rather than the rational price of $5)*

Medium - $7

Large - $9

Result: This upsells more people into the medium option because now, *most people who would normally get a small, will get a medium.*

Bottom Line: If you have a lot of customers buying small, you can bump them to mediums. If you have a lot of customers buying the medium, bump them to large. If you have a lot of customers buying large, raise *all* your prices.

Upsell Guarantees, Warranties, and Insurance. Many businesses offer guarantees on products. Many businesses offer warranties on products. Many businesses offer insurance on products. You can upsell all of them. *So instead of doing it for free, just add 5–50% onto the price in exchange for a guarantee that your thing does what you say it will.* Ex: An art studio used to replace damaged portraits at no charge. I told them to start asking customers if they would pay an extra 10% for it. Now, 30% of customers buy stuff the art studio used to give away for free. Pure profit baby.

Summary

- Your Attraction Offer reveals a problem. Upsells (whatever you offer next) solves it.

- Use The Classic Upsell for *immediate* problems revealed by your previous offer.

- Asking "you don't want anything else do you?" gets people to agree by saying no. It works.

- Increase the chance customers take upsells by giving them access to it as soon as possible.

- Give away bonuses that create an upsell opportunity. A great way to make more cash.

- To get more chances to upsell customers, make BAMFAM a way of life.

- You can have as many upsell offers as you want as long as you solve problems.

- You lose nothing by offering to solve someone's problem.

- If it makes sense for your business, you can charge for guarantees, warranties, or insurance rather than give them away for free.

FREE GIFT: Watch The Classic Upsell Video Training [No Opt-in Required]

The first upsell everyone should learn is the classic upsell. There are a bunch of tiny tips that can make a big difference. I made a video training to make sure you didn't miss any of tiny details. You can watch it for free at acquisition.com/training/money. QR code for easy fast access.

Menu Upsell

You don't need that…you need this

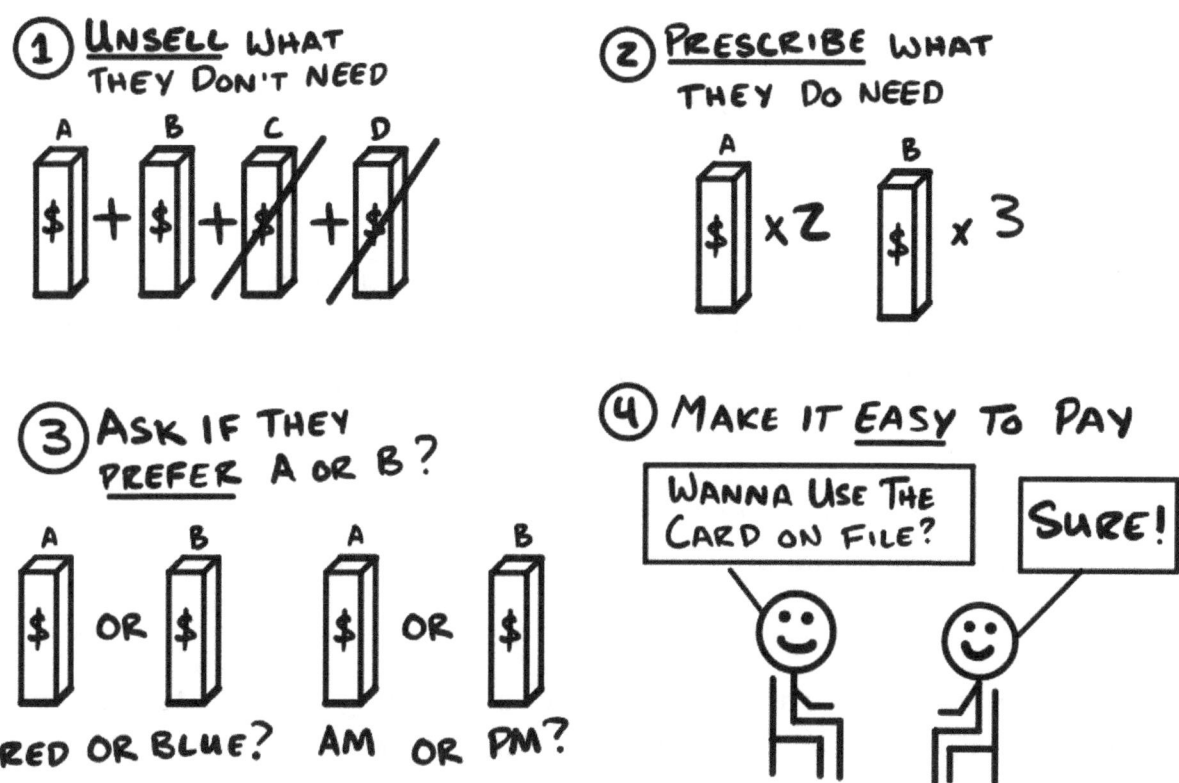

December 2013.

People kept joining the gym like normal, but nobody cared about my supplements. I read somewhere keeping shelves full got more people to buy. So I stocked my shelves with all the labels in a perfect row. It didn't work. I also read if I told everyone about the cool science they would buy. That didn't work either. I got a few pitty purchases from loyal members, but I was doing something seriously wrong. *Why do I suck so much?*

On a particularly rough day, I had nineteen nutrition consults, and nobody bought anything. It was miserable. Then, appointment number twenty came in. She had a nice purse and a big diamond ring on her hand. *If I can't sell her, I should just quit trying.* But then I remembered…*I've got $5,000 in inventory on that shelf—I've gotta figure this out!*

We went through her nutrition consultation and I started getting nervous. I got so nervous I forgot my script. And rather than blabbing about science stuff, I just asked "You've got a protein shake for breakfast, do you like chocolate or vanilla?"

"Which one's your favorite?" She asked.

"Chocolate."

"Great. I'll take one of those."

Wait, what just happened? I didn't talk about the benefits or anything. I just asked what she wanted…and she told me! Taking the hint, I moved to the next item.

"Do you want kiwi or strawberry lemonade pre-workout?"—then I remembered her last question—"…I like strawberry lemonade."

Smiling, "Great, I'll take that one."

I had more products, but selling two was a record and I didn't want to scare her away. I still had to ask for money. So I grabbed her membership contract that already had her card on it and asked "You just wanna use the card we have on file?"

"Yep—that's fine."

After that conversation, I sold the next twenty customers in a row. At the end of the day, I stared at my empty shelf in disbelief. *I know how to sell supplements.*

Takeaway: I stumbled on two tactics that changed my upsell game forever. First, the <u>A/B Upsell</u>—I ask *which product they prefer* rather than *whether* they want the product at all. Second, asking *if they want to use the card on file* rather than asking them to take out their card again. I still use both to this day.

August 2014.

Now, I closed sales left and right. Bing bang boom. Now it wasn't exactly big stuff, but I was selling consistently. Every month I'd start another group of challengers. And like clockwork, I'd upsell $5,000 to $10,000 worth of supplements. Not bad for a day's work!

But one day, I had a lady who just wouldn't stop asking questions. She kept wanting more information. How to take them. How many. When. What times. What if she was working. What if she was at home. What if she was at the gym. She was relentless. I was gonna be late for my next consult. So finally, I just wrote step-by-step instructions on the back of some scratch paper. *Take one of these at night. Take two of these after lunch. Drink this after your workout. Yada yada yada.*

I walked her through what I wrote and asked. "Make sense?"

Nodding. "Thanks!" She grabbed the paper and left.

My next appointment had overheard our entire conversation. As soon as she sat down, she asked "do you think you could write it out like you did for that other lady?" I tried not to let out a sigh—*I failed.* I was gonna be late for my next consult *again.*

But, I did as she asked. This time, I wrote the instructions right on the order form. Next to each item, I wrote how much to take and when. And because I didn't want to push my appointments back another fifteen minutes, I just went for the upsell.

"I got all your instructions here, do you want to just use the card on file?" I asked.

"Yea that's fine."

Hot diggity dawg. She just bought all those products…and I didn't even ask her anything. *I told her.* And she did it. Like magic.

I did this from that day forward, and my 30-day profits skyrocketed.

Takeaway: I learned *detailed* and *personalized* instructions upsell more people than vague and general suggestions. I call this <u>prescription upselling</u>.

November 2016.

By now, I was on the road launching other people's gyms. And that included selling supplements. I sold thousands of people. I'd see 40 to 50 a day. Two people. Every 30 minutes. 12 hours straight. My supplement-selling marathons alone covered the flight there, my hotel *and* advertising costs. I got so good I'd run out of stuff to sell. Today was one of those days.

I just sold a lady the last of four different products. In situations like this, I'd sell whatever I had left to the next customer. But before I could pitch, she blurted out, "Can I just get what she got?" *Oh boy.*

I said "Sorry, I just ran out. But honestly, you can get something close at the shop down the street for about $20 less. It's not as good, but it'll do OK for the first month. Cool?"

"Thank you so much for helping me out." She seemed so grateful. It felt good. So I continued *unselling.*

"This other thing, same story. Again, not as good, but it'll get you through the first month." She seemed so happy. I couldn't stop myself now. I started unselling stuff *I wasn't going to sell her anyways.*

"You're not trying to gain weight, right?" I joked.

"Oh god no!" she laughed.

"Okay great. You won't be needing this," crossing out the weight-gainer shake. "Oh, and you aren't trying to boost your testosterone right?"

"No haha. I don't think so," she said.

"Great. You won't be needing this either." I crossed it out. Then, I started making suggestions from what I had left. "Okay. So you're gonna need to take two of these…three of these…" and I went on. She loved it *and bought without hesitation.*

Takeaway: I went out of my way to cross out what she didn't need. And this built enough goodwill to upsell what she *did.* Later, I kept products *just to cross them out!* I call this process <u>unselling</u>.

Description

In a Menu Upsell, you tell customers which options they don't need. Then, tell them what they do need, their preferences, *and* how to get their value from it. Menu Upsells combine up to four tactics: Unselling, Prescription Upselling, A/B Upselling, and Card On File.

First, I <u>unsell</u> what customers don't need.

Second, I <u>prescribe</u> what they do need.

Third, I ask their preferences between <u>A and B</u>.

Last, I make buying easy by asking if they want to use the <u>card on file</u>.

Unselling. You unsell by telling customers what they don't need so that you can emphasize what they do. Here, instead of asking ***if*** they want to buy it or not, you explain ***what they don't need*** as a way to ***get them excited about what they do.*** Unsells vary based on the customer's needs. When some options work best, you can cross out the rest. After telling them what they <u>don't</u> need…

Prescription Upsell. We tell them what they <u>do</u> need. Prescription Upsells work well when offering a choice is inconvenient and you have only one thing that solves the problem. Prescription upselling has two important components. First, you have to explain how it integrates with offers they already bought. Second, you personalize and detail how to maximize its value. Here, instead of asking ***if*** they want to buy it or not, you explain ***how to use it*** as if they already have. Again, we remove the option of not buying to lower the chance they don't buy. And once I have told them exactly how they're going to use everything…

A/B Upsell. We ask them their preferences. A/B Upsells work for *multiple offers that solve the same problem.* You make A/B Upsells by asking their preference. Instead of asking ***if*** customers wanted to buy a product, yes or no, we ask which product they ***prefer:*** A or B. Either choice results in an upsell. Basically, when you give people the option to not buy, some don't buy. So, I give the option to pick between buying two similar things. Once they know what they're buying and how they're gonna use it, I suggest the easiest way for them to pay…

Card On File. A cherry on top of all this upsell goodness. I literally ask, "Do you want to use the card on file?" Here, instead of asking ***if*** they want to pay or not, you ***refer*** to ways they already have. This gets more people to buy because it lowers the "hidden costs" of buying. Picking which card to use. Taking it out. Being reminded of ugly buying decisions in the past. Even the hassle of buying stuff in a rush…and who knows how many more. Just know if you make it easy for people to buy, more people will.

<u>This took me ten years to learn. May you get the same value in ten minutes.</u>

Examples

<u>Massage Therapist</u>

- *Unsell:* We have a lymphatic massage available, but you're not pregnant or just out of surgery right? So we can cross that out.

- *Prescribe:* Since your shoulder hurts we'll heat you up first, then hit your trigger points, and after that, we'll do some dynamic stretches.

- *A/B:* So would you rather do it before work or on the way home?

- *Card On File:* Wanna just use the card on file?

Dog Food

- *Unsell:* You're not gonna need this small bag or this puppy stuff—you've got a big dog! You don't need these vitamins either because the food already contains them.

- *Prescribe:* You're also gonna wanna give your dog one of these joint chews at each meal. And every 90 days, give them one of these wafers for heartworms. Also, make sure to bring him back next month. Let's get that booked now.

- *A/B:* So does your dog prefer beef or chicken flavor?

- *Card On File:* Wanna just use the card on file?

Digital Product

- *Unsell:* You don't need all eight courses yet. You just need to solve X, Y, & Z. Tell ya what. I'll send you some free stuff that'll solve problems X and Y. Then, you'll just need one course for problem Z…

- *Prescribe:* But to solve Z, you're definitely gonna wanna do the course *this* particular way. Can you put an hour a day towards it? Okay—great. This will prevent any other Z problems cropping up later.

- *A/B:* Would you rather have direct message or phone support? Okay great. And would you like to start today or Monday?

- *Card On File:* Awesome. Wanna just use the card on file?

Pro Tip: "Card On File" for first purchases—*What card do you wanna to use?*

Important Notes:

Make Anything A/B Sellable. You can turn *anything* into an A/B offer. Just to give you a few ideas…Quantity (do you want one bottle or two?), start dates (start tomorrow or Monday?), payment preference (cash or card?), flavors (chocolate or vanilla?), time slots (morning or afternoon?), media (read or listen?), delivery speeds (standard or overnight?), sizes (small or medium?), colors (black or white?), materials (paper or plastic?), personnel (John or Sara?), communication (call or text?). With some creativity, you can make *anything* an A/B upsell.

If You Make An A/B Offer, Add A Nudge. If your customers have limited experience with your products or service, give them a nudge. *"This is my favorite"* or *"X is usually a safe bet"* or *"a lot of people love this"* or *"Tuesday's sessions are a little smaller if you like that"* or *"Amy does great with high schoolers."* These one-liners really help move sales along. (Hint: If you want to move one particular product faster, *nudge* that one more.)

If You've Sold Out Of It, Take Payment And Delay Delivery. Later I learned I could just sell them stuff, order it, and set the expectation of when it will arrive. This allowed me to sell way more selection because I didn't have to carry inventory. If you run out, consider just collecting the cash and changing the delivery expectations. You'd be surprised how well this works.

Employees Love Unselling. Employees often *like* helping customers "game the system." *Let them.* Encourage employees to help customers game the system on purpose. Your employees have inside knowledge, so allow them to show customers how to get the most value out of what you have to offer. Everyone wins.

See "The 'Economist' Play" below for a visual explanation.

THE "ECONOMIST" PLAY

WITH ONLY 2 OPTIONS...

$10

$20

A

OR

A + B

MORE PEOPLE TAKE

IF WE ADD A "DECOY" 3RD OPTION AT SAME $ AS A+B...

$10

$20

$20

A

OR

B

OR

A + B

MORE PEOPLE TAKE

If You Have Two Options And Want People To Buy Both

In the late 1990's *The Economist* magazine started offering a digital subscription because more people got their news online. But, it also wanted to keep its profitable print subscription. So, thinking people would buy both, *The Economist* offered the following:

A- Digital Subscription: $59/year

B- Digital + Print Subscription: $125/year

Result: Print sales *plummeted* as customers flocked to the cheaper option. Oops.

To fix it, they added a decoy option *for the same price* as the bundle:

A- Digital Subscription: $59/year

B- Print Subscription: $125/year

C- Digital + Print Subscription: $125/year

Result: Customers now took the C - Digital + Print option $125/year.

Bottom Line: Present three options. Option A, Option B, and Option C (Both)... but you make the price of (C) the same as the more expensive option (B). So long as you price the options to preserve your margins, you make the customer's choice easy *and sell both.*

Summary Points

- Menu Upsells work best when you have multiple offers available.

- Menu Upsells combine up to four tactics:

  o <u>Unselling</u>: You tell customers what they don't need.

  o <u>Prescribing</u>: Tell them what they do need.

  o <u>A/B Offer</u>: Ask them what they prefer.

  o Last, I make buying easy by asking if they want to use the <u>Card On File</u>.

- Unselling lower-margin stuff where appropriate incentivizes higher-margin upsells.

- Encourage employees to unsell and "game the system" on purpose.

- Nudge new customers towards what makes sense for them.

FREE GIFT: Watch The Menu Upsell Training

I rarely make commands. Just do it. Watch it. I can teach a masterclass on this upsell. It's made me millions. That's it. Just go to acquisition.com/training/money. Yes, it's free. No, you won't be sorry. QR code for easy fast access.

Anchor Upsell

The only thing worse than making a $1,000 offer to a person with a $100 budget...
is making a $100 offer to someone with a $1,000 budget.

2016. After Starting Gym Launch, But Before Making Money.

I had spent my last five years showerless, in sweats and a tank top. But now I had Gym Launch, and a fashionable friend said I should look professional. "Businessmen don't wear tank tops Alex. I know the owner of a local suit shop. I'll tell him you're coming." I took his advice and went.

So, I budgeted $500 for a suit—a big purchase at the time. I walked into the suit shop and made small talk. The owner knew I was coming. *Wow.* I told him I just started a new business and wanted a "boss suit." He took my measurements, then grabbed two suits off the rack. I put the first one on.

"How's it look? How do you feel?"

I smiled. *I felt cool.* Like a rich guy. It was nice. He talked about some accessories but I didn't listen much. I was 'too cool' to listen now (ha!). *This is gonna be awesome.* He turned to talk to an employee. I flipped the price tag over so I could see it...

...*$16,000.* My face turned red. All I could think was *my friend asked the owner to make time for me and I can't even afford anything here.* I felt horrified. I kept my head down to try and hide my shock. I took a breath and looked up. I failed. He had seen me blush.

Coming to my aid he asked "Do you care about the designer much?"

"Not at all."

Almost before I finished replying, the owner whirled around and draped the next suit over my shoulders. "Try this on for size." he said.

I looked in the mirror. *Looks good.*

Then I looked down at the price tag...*$2,200.*

It wasn't $500. But it wasn't $16,000 either. Sigh of relief.

"Yea. This works. I'll take this one."

He winked and nodded. "You got it boss."

The owner sold me some socks, a handkerchief, and a shirt to go with it. All in, another $300. But, after seeing the $16,000 price tag on the first suit, *everything* seemed cheap.

***

Looking back, this wasn't the owner's first rodeo. He was a real pro. I spent five times more than I had budgeted and felt OK about it. I only later realized he used a *Price Anchor.*

Description

With Anchor Upsells, you offer premium stuff first. If the customer gasps, you offer a cheaper but acceptable alternative.

Basically, if you present your main offer, *some* people will buy it. Duh. But, if you present a premium version that's 5x–10x the price first, lots of people will say no. Then, when you present your main offer, it looks like a *much better deal.* So, more people will buy it. Aha! That's the power of Anchor Upsells.

Anchor Upsells work best when the lower-price offer has the same *core functions* as the premium one. For instance, I didn't care about the designer that much. I just needed a suit. So, compared to the $16,000 suit, the $2,200 suit was a *way better deal.*

Anchor Upsells also have two amazing bonuses. First, anchored customers spend more than they normally would. Second, *some customers still buy the super expensive thing.*

Here are the steps:

1) Present the Anchor—the really expensive thing.

2) Get "The Gasp"—expect the customer to freak out about the cost.

3) Come to the rescue—ask if they care about *what makes it premium.*

4) Present your main offer—expect the customer to feel relieved and see the *better deal.*

5) Ask how they wanna pay—*Which card do you prefer?*

Pro Tip: The Only Thing Worse Than Making A $1,000 Offer To A Person With A $100 Budget...is Making A $100 Offer To Someone With A $1,000 Budget.

In the first situation you lose $100. In the second, you lose $900. I've lost tons of customers and mountains of cash *because* customers wanted more than I had to offer. Boo. So now I always have premium upsells ready. Only a handful of customers buy them, but that handful of customers bring *big profits.* So always have premium offers *even if most people don't buy.* Remember, you won't lose customers by offering premium stuff first, *but you WILL lose money if you don't.*

Examples

<u>Local Service: Lawn Care</u>

Premium Anchor: Get my cell phone number, fancy mulch, natural pest control, bi-weekly yard maintenance—$1,000 per week

Main Offer: Get my team's number, generic mulch, normal pest control, bi-weekly yard maintenance—$200 per week

Physical Product: A Painting

Premium Anchor: Super protective packaging + 20 year insurance + gift wrapped = $1,000

Main Offer: Normal packaging + 1 year insurance + sticker = $200

Digital Product: Newsletter

Premium Anchor: All previous issues + new issues + 24hrs early = $199/mo

Main Offer: New issues only + on time = $19/mo

Important Notes

If You Treat The Anchor Like A Fake, So Will The Customer. Some people hear about this technique. Try it. Gloss over the premium offer. *And then say it doesn't work.* But if you do that, then the person never really considered it because you never really offered it. You *went through the motions.* For this to work, you need to actually sell it and they have to actually consider it. Only after they pause, hesitate, or ask for something else, do you move to the next thing.

Make A Premium Offer You Actually Want People To Buy. A friend of mine struggled to get this working. I only had to listen to one call to figure out the problem. He made up some BS that he didn't really want them to buy. So we tweaked the offer to something he would *actually* feel happy to deliver if someone paid…and they did. *Tripling his profits.* Actually present your premium offer like you *want* people to take it. And when you do, some will. And if they don't, you still anchored them.

A Proper Anchor Gets "The Gasp." When you do an anchor upsell correctly, customers will have mini panic attacks. I call this "The Gasp." Gasps used to really stress me out. But then I realized something huge. The bigger the gasp, the more they bought.

Once You Get The Gasp—Come To The Rescue. In the story, I gave "The Gasp." Then, the sales pro saved my ego by asking if I cared about the designer. When I said no, he presented the next suit. Key point: he already had the 1/8th price suit pulled before my reaction. He *knew* I would probably gasp. And if your customers don't gasp, then they probably find your premium offer reasonable…so just ask them if they wanna use the card on file (ha! Go for it!). Just don't do a gasp of your own when they say yes. You're welcome. You can buy me a beer later.

To Get More People To Buy Your Main Offer, Make It A Better Deal. Only tweak a few features from your premium offer to make your main offer. Every offer has features. Some features matter more than others. You want the primary features to stay the same. Fewer people care about secondary features, *so change those.* This allows customers to get the same primary features and a *way better deal.* Most people just want a suit. A few people want a fancy suit. A suit is the primary feature. The material, designer, etc. is secondary. After anchoring, offering the primary features for a fifth of the price makes the main offer a *great deal.*

Summary

- If you present a more expensive offer before a less expensive offer, more people will buy the less expensive offer than they would have if you had presented the less expensive offer on its own.

- Present anchor. Get gasp. Come to the rescue. Present core offer. Ask for payment.

- For the most effective anchor, make your premium offer 5–10x more expensive.

- Anchored customers spend a bit more than they plan to.

- Don't treat the anchor like a fake, or the customer will too. You lose trust *and* waste time.

- Important: Some customers will buy the premium offer.

- Expensive premium offers add outsized profits with fewer sales.

- The main offer and the premium offer should have the same primary features.

- The premium offer has different secondary—aka 'premium'—features.

- After anchoring, offering the primary features for a fifth of the price makes the main offer a *great deal.* It gives them 'basically the same thing' for *way* less.

FREE GIFT: Anchor Upsell Training

This thing can help you make insane amounts of profit overnight. Truly life changing. I made an additional video for you on it. Don't worry, it's free. Watch it at acquisition.com/training/money. I put a QR code for easy fast access.

Rollover Upsell

Wanna just roll it forward?

June 2014.

I had been running a Win Your Money Back Offer (Attraction Offer #1) at my gym for the last year. A $600 fitness program where members could win their money back—*if they hit a goal.* It crushed. I sold tons of them.

But there was a problem. Good gyms have lots of recurring revenue. *I had none.* Most winners put their $600 toward three months of membership. Fine. But then they churned out before their first out-of-pocket payment. So I essentially sold "buy six weeks get three months free." Then, they'd leave. Not fine.

That $600 thing was my *only* source of income. So even though I got a bunch of people in the door, my revenue started at zero every month. It was stressful. I had to figure out a better way to boost profit.

That's when my friend Justin posted how he added *another* hundred members to his recurring revenue. He also attracted customers with a Win Your Money Back Offer. But there was one difference: my customers left, and *his kept buying stuff.* So, I invited myself over to spy on him. He was totally cool with it. I spent two days there. He and I ran some things differently, but nothing that explained why he was doing *so much* better than me.

"Do you get lots of people winning their money back?"

"Yeah," he said.

"Then how do you deal with all the free time you have to give away?"

"Free time? Ha! I just *roll over* their winnings into a year long membership."

"What?"

"Yea—we have to do that so we can spread the money out."

"Spread the money? What are you talking about?"

"Seriously? What—you give it all up front?" He didn't wait for me to answer. "We just give them fifty bucks off per month for a year."

"So even though they won their money back, *they start paying immediately?*"

"Of course. I don't want people not paying. What sort of business doesn't have paying customers??" He laughed. "They still get their money back…it just takes a year."

Boom. This was it. The missing link in my Money Model.

***

This *one* thing, the Rollover Upsell, changed my life, thousands of gym owners' lives, and the lives of our customers. The Rollover Upsell changed *everything*.

Now, instead of *hoping* customers spend money again, I roll over the cost of what they just bought *toward the next thing*. And when paired with more expensive offers, it skyrockets 30-day profits.

And although I learned the Rollover Upsell this way, you don't need a Win Your Money Back attraction offer to use it. <u>You can Rollover Upsell *anyone anything*.</u> (Even stuff people bought at other businesses…mwahaha).

Description

Rollover Upsells credit some or all of a customer's previous purchases toward your next offer. And this—in my experience—gets *way more* people to take it. So once I know how much credit to give, I figure out three things: *who* to upsell, *what* to upsell, and *how* to roll over the credit.

<u>For the *who*,</u> I use Rollover Upsells in four situations:

First, to re-engage customers who left a while ago.

Second, to rescue upset customers as a better alternative to a refund.

Third, to 'rescue' *other people's* upset customers.

Fourth, to upsell regular customers.

For the *what,* remember, you can upsell *more of what they just got, something better,* or *something new and different.* To make money: Roll their credit over to something more expensive.

For the *how,* you can apply all or part of the discount up front or spread it over time.

Examples of Rollover Upsells

Chiropractor: *Re-engage old patients with a "Winback" Campaign*

<u>Who</u>: Customers With Six Months Since Last Purchase <u>What</u>: New Plan <u>How</u>: Up front.

Reach out to your old patients. Look at their purchase history. Offer to apply some or all of their past purchases towards something more expensive than what they bought.

Ex: *"Hi Mrs. Banks, I wanted to give you your money back, do you have a minute? Great, yea. I wanted to see how your back pain is going? Oh, I'm sorry to hear that. Well, I have some good news. As a way of saying thank you, I want to give you $500 of your money back as credit towards staying pain-free for good. Is that of any interest? Great…let's get you in…"*

Dentist: *Save Your Own Upset Customer With Rollover Upsell*

<u>Who</u>: Upset Customer <u>What</u>: Teeth Whitening <u>How</u>: Front Load $200 Credit.

The person pays $200 for teeth cleaning but doesn't think their teeth got whiter. We explain they need more to get more and upsell into a teeth whitening package which includes multiple sessions, an at-home kit, and multiple deep cleanings. You offer to credit the $200 they paid for the cleaning towards the whitening package.

Software: *Rescue (*Cough* Steal) Other People's Upset Customers*

<u>Who</u>: Competitors' customers <u>What</u>: Service agreement <u>How</u>: Rollover cost to break old agreement.

You find competitors' upset customers and credit the customers' old purchases with them towards a new purchase with you. Roll over the amount they owe with them as credit towards a longer agreement with you.

Ex: *"Hi John, I saw your negative review on their product and it really upset me. To make it up to you, I'll credit whatever payments you have left with them to switch to ours. This way, you don't lose a thing and you start getting the benefits now. Fair enough?"*

Membership: *Spread First Purchase Over a Term*

<u>Who</u>: Current customers <u>What</u>: 12-month membership <u>How</u>: Spread out first purchase.

Somebody buys a small block of service or membership time. As soon as they do, you can offer to apply the entire amount towards more time—like 12 months. I can do the rollover upsell at any time, I just prefer to do it right then. When you do, you take the first purchase's cost and apply it as a discount over the longer agreement. For example, a $600 first purchase makes a $50 per month rollover discount for 12 months.

Important Notes.

Use Rollover Offers To Attract New Customers. For example, you roll over some or all of what customers paid somebody else *towards your thing.* You can find leads for this by scraping contact information from negative product reviews where available. Voila—a hot new list of leads who need what you have. Bonus: Create a way for people to complain about products in your industry (think any media where people can leave comments). Then, Rollover Upsell all of them. Nasty.

Do Rollover Upsells *before* refunding. This has saved me tons of customers and cash. If you did a bad job (hey, it happens), roll over for a 'do over.' And if they want something different, roll over their purchase toward that thing instead.

Previous Customers Are Still Customers. Upsell Them. Reach out to old customers (6+ months since last purchase). Look at how much they paid before. Decide how much you're willing to roll over. Offer it. Actually do this. I called these "winback campaigns." I made personalized videos for 200 past customers offering them $4,000 of credit to return. We got about 20% to take the offer. One day of recording videos got us an extra ~$1,900,000 of annual revenue. Worth It.

Add Urgency To Rollover Upsells. Make Them One-Time Only. If you're spicy, make the moment you present the offer the time to take it. A once-in-a-customer-lifetime offer. *They don't get to sleep on it.* And yes, I know they might not expect it. That's the point! You want to surprise and delight. So if they want the credit, they've gotta take it *now*. If not, no big deal. They can still pay full price later.

How To Price Your Rollover Upsell. To make money on a discounted offer, you must have profit left after you discount it. Since I prefer to make a profit, I try to make the upsell offer at least four times more than their rollover credit. So even if I apply the whole amount of the first purchase, it discounts 25% *at most*. Remember, the rules of discounting apply. Bigger discounts make you less profit per sale, but they get more sales.

You Don't Need To Credit The Entire Amount Of Their First Purchase. You can roll over as much or as little of the first purchase you choose. I roll over whatever amount I think would incentivize them to buy the next thing. Test to find the sweet spot.

My "Famous" Gift Card Play. You can use the Rollover Upsell as an Attraction Offer for new *and* current customers by advertising gift cards for 90%+ off. Ex: $200 Gift Cards for $20. Limit them to two per customer and say *they can only use them on other people.* They buy them as gifts and give them to their friends. This makes it a great holiday offer.

When customers buy the gift card, ask them who they want to make it out to and if they'll make an introduction. Then, when they come in, roll their gift card over. Make the *value* of the gift card 20% of the price of whatever you want to sell next. In our example, we sell a $200 gift card for $20. Then, apply that $200 value to an offer with at least a $1,000 price tag. People pay you to refer their friends. It's pretty great. Plus, you get some pocket change from unused gift cards.

Summary Points

- Rollover Upsells credit some or all of a customer's previous purchases toward your next offer.

- To do Rollover Upsells, figure out who to upsell, what to upsell, and how to roll credit over.

- Who to upsell: old customers, upset customers, other people's upset customers, current customers.

- What to upsell: more of something, something better, something new or different. Just make sure you make a profit after applying the credit.

- How to roll credit over: Full or partial purchase price. Given up front or spread out.

- Price your next offer *at least* 4x higher than the credit. This makes a 25% discount.

- To get more takers, add urgency. Make your Rollover Upsell a one-time only offer.

FREE GIFT: Rollover Upsell Training

This is the upsell I use most frequently. It has elegant urgency built in + goodwill. I made a video for you going over some of the scripting so you can see me do it. It's free. No opt-in required. Watch it at acquisition.com/training/money. I put a QR code for easy fast access.

Upsell Offers Conclusion

Solve rich people problems, they pay better.

Anytime you offer something *next*, you upsell. Upsells play a key role in Money Models by getting more cash from customers *faster* than you otherwise would have. And if your Attraction Offer already covers the costs of getting customers and delivering—*more money ain't a bad thing*.

I showed you the four most powerful Upsells I use: The Classic Upsell, Menu Upsells, Anchor Upsells, and Rollover Upsells. They are core to my business success. Upsells change everything. Many businesses go from burning cash to printing it—*overnight*.

But, as you know, business isn't all sunshine and rainbows. Sometimes, *people say no*. This leads us to the next component of a *$100M Money Model*—Downsell Offers: *what to do when they say no…*

SECTION IV:
DOWNSELL OFFERS

What to offer when they say no.

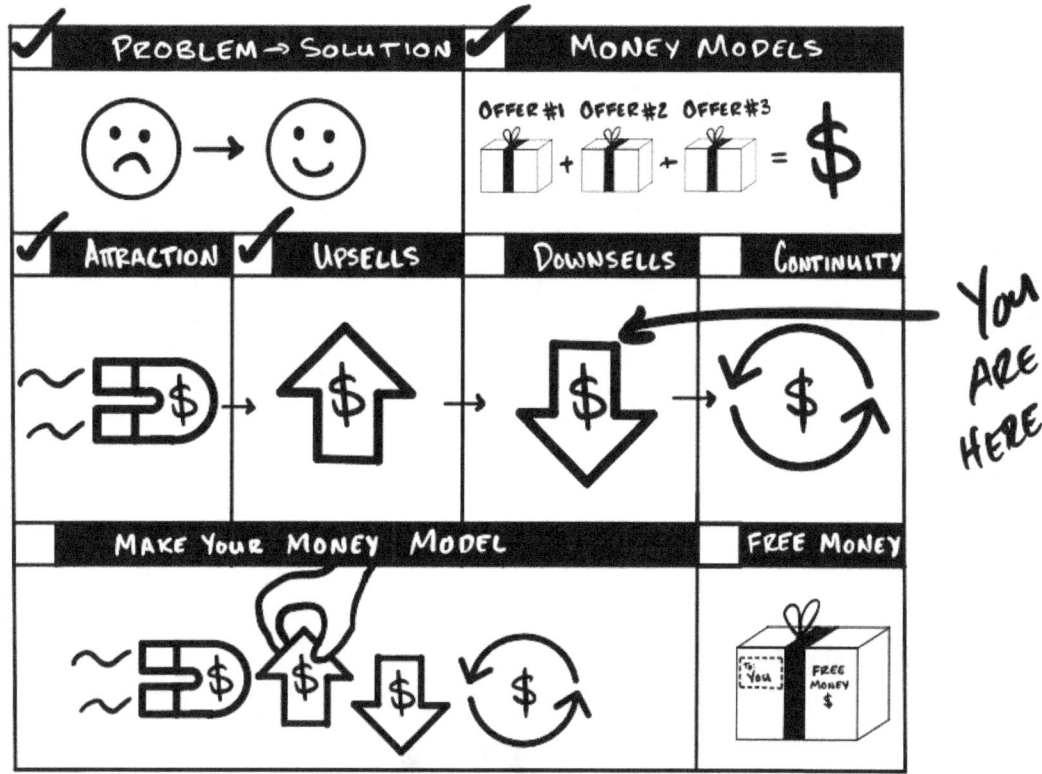

In the last section, we used Upsell Offers to get people to buy more stuff. If we did a good job, we've turned a profit too. Another step forward! Awesome…but what if they say no? → *We downsell them.*

Downselling tweaks the original offer to find the highest value solution *for the customer's budget.* So any offer you make after someone says 'no' is a downsell.

I downsell in two ways. I change <u>how they pay</u> or *what they get.* For how they pay, I balance how much they pay now with how much they pay over time. For what they get, I change quantity, quality, or offer something different.

First, we cover my rules of downselling—*they apply to all my downsell processes.* Then, when we dive into individual offers, you can hit the ground running and downsell like a pro.

How <u>Not</u> To Downsell—A Real Story From A Friend.

*"I was buying a car and the salesman tried to upsell car insurance. The cost of the insurance when he first started was $5,000. I said no. But then, he lowered the price. And I said no again. He kept lowering the price until the **same insurance he first offered** for $5,000 was now only $400! I still said no. At first I said no because it was too much money, but by the end I said no because I didn't trust the guy. The entire experience felt dirty. Then I wondered, was he ripping me off on the car too? Now, I didn't want to buy the car from him either!"*

People lower the price to close a sale. But even if you close this one sale, the customer will question every price you offer from that point going forward… and whoever they tell. You trade trust for a buck. Not worth it.

Note: You can offer something different for less. You just can't offer the *same thing* for less. If he had offered *different* insurance for less, rather than *the same* insurance for less, he probably would've kept her trust and closed the sale.

The Rules of Downselling

Downsells

Remember, They Said No To *This* Offer, Not *All* Offers. Sometimes (a lotta times) people say no…*and that's OK*. Just because they rejected *this offer* does not mean they rejected *you*. It hurts when someone rejects you. I get it. But see it for what it is—an opportunity to find out what they really want, and profit from it. Instead of hiding your head in the sand, stand your ground and make another offer. *No means no for this thing, not no for everything.*

Downsells Are Trades. When downselling, you work with the customer to find combinations of giving and getting until you get a match. *If you're gonna give something, get something.*

Personalize, Don't Pressure. Figure out what they like and don't like. Then, offer more of what they like and less of what they don't—*with a price to match.* You're personalizing here. If someone refuses my large soda upsell, I can offer alternatives. I could ask if they want a small, a juice, or a coffee. Am I being offensive by asking? Absolutely not. In fact, if I can better serve them, it would be offensive *not to.*

Offer The Same Things In New Ways. In a perfect world, you've got tons of different things to sell so everyone buys something. In the real world, you limit downsells to what you've got. Otherwise, you create a hundred businesses' worth of products (and problems). A silly choice. So just think of downselling more like a hundred ways to offer the stuff you already have.

Don't Drop Your Price Just To Get Somebody To Buy. First off, dropping your price is not really downselling, *it's discounting.* If someone wants what you have, and just doesn't want to pay the price—tough cookies. On the other hand, you *can* offer them to pay less *now* and more money over time—a payment plan. But, whatever you do, don't change the price just to get someone to buy because…

Customers Talk About Price. By all means, test prices. Plan to offer your thing at a specific price, to a specific number of people, *ahead of time.* That's way different than charging somebody less in the moment just because you felt scared of losing the sale *in the moment.* Customers talk. If they find out someone got the same thing for less *"just because"* —you'll upset people. And it also becomes an ethical problem, at least to me. Avoid it.

Next Up…

I use three simple and brutally effective downsell processes:

- Payment Plan Downsells (*how they pay*)

- Trial With Penalty (*how they pay*)

- Feature Downsells (*what they get*)

These downsell processes boost 30-day profit even further. They do it by making even more sales when customers would have said no. And I love them because with just a couple tweaks, you can fit them into your business and reap the rewards today.

FREE GIFT: Downsell Offers Video Training

People say no. Don't get flustered. Get focused. Know what you're going to offer next. I made a video to go over this chapter in detail for you. Enjoy it free at acquisition.com/training/money. I put a QR code for easy fast access.

Payment Plan Downsells

How much can you put down today?

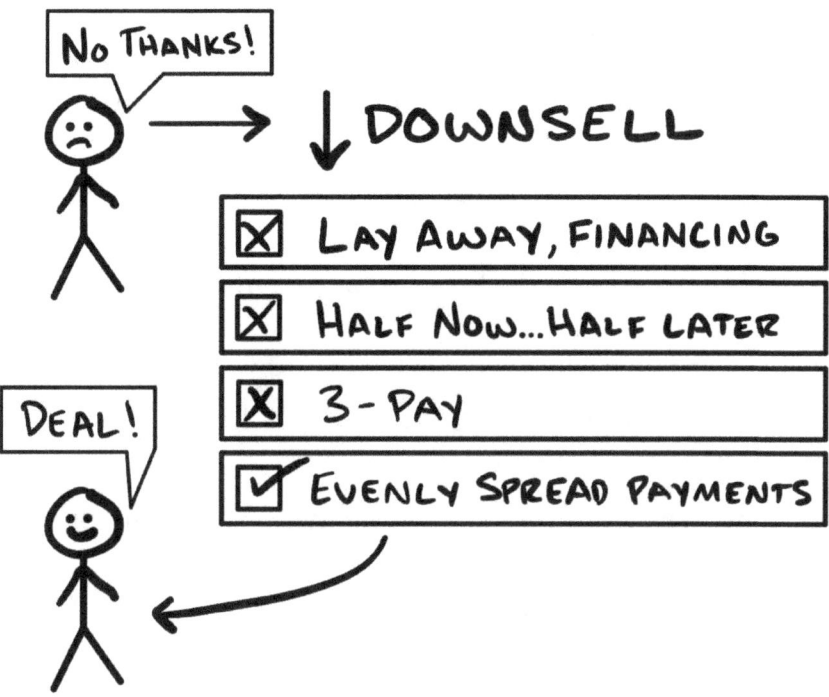

August 2013.

It was my first real month in business. I had exactly one month's rent in savings left to my name…and *I had never gotten a stranger to give me money.* And now, I had to get dozens of strangers to give me money in the next few weeks—just to keep the lights on.

I only made a few sales the first week. If I kept that up, it meant going hungry very soon. I had nightmares about going back home a failure. The idea was unbearable. I got desperate.

The next morning a lead walked in and I went through my normal pitch. She said "I can't afford it." Normally, I'd just give up. But, I *really* needed the money. So in my desperation I blurted out "OK, when do you get paid?"

"The first."

"Okay, just put half down now, and half when you get paid."

"I can't afford that either."

"Okay—do you really wanna do this program?"

"Yeah, I do."

"What if you do three payments and just put a third down today?"

"I still can't do it."

"Hmm… What *can* you do?

"Honestly, nothing. But I can pay for the whole thing on the first."

My rent was due on the fifth. *Bingo*. "Sounds good. Just give me your card and I'll charge it on the second. That work?"

"Yea—great!"

Two weeks later. I ran the card. *And it worked.* My first ever payment plan—a success. Hallelujah.

***

Payment Plan Downsells work no matter how many zeroes the price tag has. I've made tens of millions of dollars with them and I still use them to this day. But, payment plans are a gamble. So you have to know how to use them. I know *how* to use them and I'll show you exactly how.

Payment plans are a gamble because they can make money in one way, *but they can lose money in two*. They make you more money when you get more customers and those customers complete their payments. They make you less money when people cancel before you turn a profit. You lose the most when people who would have paid in full take a payment plan—and cancel early.

This chapter maximizes how much money you make from payment plans and minimizes the money you lose. I take the bet when I know I'll win. With this playbook, you can too.

Description

When most people think "downsell," they think of a lower amount, lower quality, cheaper, and so on. Fair enough. But I like to downsell by offering the same product again. I know it sounds crazy, but hear me out. Instead of offering a different thing, I spread the cost by charging some of it up front and putting the rest into scheduled payments. I call this a Payment Plan Downsell. Let's go over how they work.

Many people reject offers because they "cost too much." Sometimes true. But in response to this, business owners and other sales professionals will immediately discount or sell cheaper stuff *just to get people to say yes*. However, a *huge* percentage of the time "it costs too much" *really means* "this costs too much *up front*." In other words, people think discounts work because people pay less for the product. But when you peel it back a layer, it's really because they pay less *in the moment*. So Payment Plans get the best of both worlds. They get more buyers because customers pay less in the moment. But they also boost your profits because customers still pay full price over time.

My Payment Plan Downsell process takes up to seven steps. The process shifts from getting paid more up front to more over time. I stop when they buy. Here are the steps:

1) Reward for paying in full rather than punish for paying over time

2) Offer 3rd-party financing, credit card, layaway options

3) Offer half now, half later

4) Check to see if they still want the thing

5) Offer to split into three payments

6) Offer evenly spread payments

7) Offer a Free Trial

Let's go through them in order.

Example Of Payment Plan Downsell Process

Step 1) Reward For Paying In Full Rather Than Punish For Paying Over Time. If I take on the risk of a payment plan, I increase the price. Normal businesses do it by charging interest. But, I do it by offering a discount *if they pay in full*.

Think about how businesses normally charge interest—they basically say…"*It's $10 if you get it right now, but it's $15 if you pay over time because we charge $5 in interest.*" No fun.

Instead, I say "*It's $15…but it's $10 if you prepay it. You save $5…that's what most people do.*" To do this, I present the price *with interest included*. Then, I offer prepayment as a way to get a discount. This way, we make the offer friendlier *and* benefit from a price anchor. Same math, but feels better.

If they say no, I start downselling. But, even still. I try to get paid first…

Step 2) Offer 3rd-Party Financing, Credit Card, and Layaway Options.

3rd-Party Financing: This means another company pays me now and the customer has a payment plan *with that other company.* Car dealers do this all the time. The dealer gets money from the financing company today, and the customer pays the financing company tomorrow.

Note: It takes work to get 3rd-party financing set up. But, totally worth the effort.

Credit Card: Just ask "would you rather I decide your payment terms or you decide?" They say they'd prefer to decide. When they do, I tell them to use a credit card. That way I get paid today and they can pay the credit card company over time. It's wild to me that this reframe works. But, it does. I don't judge, I do.

Layaway: Layaway means paying off the product *before* getting it. Customers can make as many installments as they want. They can take any reasonable amount of time to pay. But, they only get the product *after they've paid in full.* This is *by far* the most flexible for them and lowest risk for us.

If they say no to these, I move to step 3.

Step 3) Offer 'Half Now, Half Later.' I start by asking *"When's the next time you get paid?"* After, I ask *"Wanna just put half down today and the rest down when you get paid?"* If they can't do that, I ask *"What's the most you can put down today?"* When they offer an amount say, *"Great. We'll put that down today and put the rest when you get paid. Fair enough?"* I like scheduling payments off of paychecks since most people get paid every two weeks. This boosts 30-day profit way more than monthly payments.

If they can't do those...I pause to make sure they actually want it.

Step 4) Check To See If They Still Want The Thing. No payment plan will satisfy a customer who doesn't want the thing. So, make sure the person actually wants your thing before putting more effort into selling it. I might say something like *"Got it. So money is tight right now. Real quick. I want to make sure. On a scale from 1–10 how bad do you wanna do this?"* If they say 8 or above, keep offering payment plans and say *"Awesome. Don't worry. We're gonna figure out a way to make this happen for you."* If they say 7 or below, ask *"Why not a 10?"* and then, say something like *"You're right. I think we may have something that could be a better fit for you."* Then you sell them something different (Feature Downsells—a little later).

Step 5) Offer To Split Into Three Payments. If they said 8–10 on the scale, I downsell from half down to a third down. I offer a three-payment option: ⅓ now and ⅓ on the next two paychecks—or—⅓ now and ⅓ the next two months.

Step 6) Offer Evenly Spread Payments. If they still can't manage it, I evenly spread payments over the rest of their service. For instance, Gym Launch was sixteen weeks long, so I charged them each week (sixteen times in total). If that still creates problems, I move to step 7.

Step 7) Offer A Free Trial. I offer Free Trials in a special way. So, I dedicated the next chapter to it. But, the sale ends here. At least for now.

This Payment Plan Downsell process makes up to *nine* offers. And if you think that sounds crazy, you're probably making way less money and serving way fewer customers than you could.

Important Notes

"Seesaw" Downselling. If you prefer fewer steps, or have less experienced salespeople, then you can use this payment plan downsell process. Instead of asking for the full amount, just ask *"Would you rather have giant monthly payments or tiny ones?"* They'll say tiny. Then you say *"It normally costs XXX. And if you prepay it today, you get a huge discount and zero monthly payments. That work?"* This frames the payment plan as negative and highlights the benefits of prepaying.

Then, if they say they can't afford it, say the more they put down now, the lower their monthly payments. *"If you can't afford it up front, I totally get it. We'll simply adjust the down payment until you get a monthly rate you like."* This still incentivizes bigger down payments to get their monthly payments lower. If they still say no, ask if they still want the product. If they do, pull your chair to their side of the table and walk them through the options. The sale becomes a team effort. Straightforward.

Payment Plans Have Built-In Upsells: Make periodic offers for the original paid-in-full-discount during their payment plan. If they pay off the balance, they can still get the original 'prepay discount.' This works exceptionally well. Customers forget they have the option. So when we give it to them, some jump at the opportunity. Also, give your sales guys the same bonus to close the balance to incentivize follow up. And remember, *if you give people the option to pay slower, they will pay slower. If you incentivize them to pay faster, they will pay faster.* So if you want them to pay faster, give them a good reason to.

Get Fewer Declined Payments. Align payment schedules with paycheck schedules. If you charge on days people get paid, they have a higher chance of paying. Also, people's paychecks get deposited at different times, so if at first it gets declined, run it a few times that day. I learned this strategy from John (my early mentor). I often recoup a third of my declined payments by adding this little process.

How To Make Sure Payment Plans Make You Money. After implementing payment plans, your close rate should increase. Duh. But, if the number of paid-in-fulls goes down, you have a problem. You've just put people who would've paid in full on payment plans! So, *you want to close more appointments overall but with the same percentage of appointments paying in full.*

Ex: If I talk to ten leads, I might sell three. If I have a downsell, I might sell three more (for a total of six). So, in the second scenario, I get my up front cash from the first three *and* the payments from the second three. This makes sure downsells properly increase your 30-day profits.

Another Reason To Start High Before Working Your Way Down. Profitwell (a company that manages subscriptions) reported churn data from 14,000 businesses. They uncovered this valuable gem. Across *all businesses*, the billing cadence affected monthly churn.

Monthly (12x per year) billing resulted in 10.7% monthly cancellation rates.

Quarterly (4x per year) billing resulted in 5% monthly cancellation rates.

Annual (1x per year) billing resulted in 2% monthly cancellations.

I already present pricing in order of most cash up front to least. It just so happens this also makes customers more valuable over the long term. So start high (fewer bigger payments) and work your way down.

Bottom Line: Changing how customers pay can have a *massive* difference in how long they stay. We go in more depth on continuity and churn in Section V: Continuity Offers.

Summary Points

- Payment Plan Downsells spread the cost of a product by charging some of it up front and putting the rest into scheduled payments.

- Payment Plans get more buyers like discounts, but can also boost profits because they agree to pay the full price over time.

- Payment Plans only grow your business if they get more customers and those customers actually pay.

- Step 1) Present at full price then offer a discount if they pay in full.

- Step 2) 3rd-party financing, then credit card option, then layaway option.

- Step 3) Split the payment in two. Schedule on their paycheck dates.

- Step 4) Ask if they still want the product on a scale of 1–10. You want 8 or greater.

- Step 5) Split the payment in three. Schedule on their paycheck dates or monthly.

- Step 6) Schedule equal payments across a specified amount of time.

- Step 7) Offer a Free Trial in exchange for putting a card down. Covered in the next chapter.

- "Seesaw" Downselling gradually shifts from paid-in-full to equal payments.

- Payment plan upsell: they get the original discount price if they pay the balance today.

- Align payment schedules with paycheck schedules to get fewer declined payments.

At the end of all this, if someone *still* refuses to pay anything, then we offer them a Free Trial in exchange for their card. But it's not an ordinary Free Trial. I do it in a special way. It took me years to perfect it. So that's where we go next. *You're gonna love it.*

FREE GIFT: Downsell Offers Video Training

Properly designed payment plans almost always make you more sales and more money. I recorded myself actually doing the step downs so you can model them for whatever you sell. For those of you who like to learn in multiple formats (which I recommend), you can watch it at acquisition.com/training/money. I put a QR code for easy fast access.

SCAN ME

Trial With Penalty

If you do X, Y, Z, I'll let you start for free.

Spring 2018.

Gym Launch was scaling fast. With 100 employees and counting, Leila needed better HR solutions to manage it all. After months of sales calls with prospective HR companies, she found one she liked. And to my surprise, it wasn't anything special—it looked like all the others.

"Yeah, the software is complicated," she said. "But they got me."

"Seriously? How did they manage that?"

"They had a trial offer with a weird spin. It was pretty smart."

"What did they offer?"

"They said if I did their training I'd get free onboarding. But, if I skipped the training I'd have to pay for it!"

"So what did you do?"

"I went through the training of course."

"So they took your credit card, you did the training—*then you didn't have to pay for the onboarding?*"

"Yep!" she smirked. "And now I can actually use the complicated software too."

Lightbulb moment.

"Wait…you said no. Then, they downsold you a free trial on the condition that they could *penalize* you if you *didn't* use it?"

"Basically. I mean, it makes sense. It forced me to learn, and now I don't want to learn anyone else's complicated software…so we're sticking with them!"

"You're right. That is pretty smart."

***

The software company used Trial With Penalty as their *Attraction* offer—but I prefer to *downsell* trials. So, I only downsell the trial if they say no to my first offer. And if you do it the way I'm about to show you, it only changes what they pay *today*—not how much they pay *in total*.

Description

In a Trial With Penalty offer, customers can try your product or service for free *so long as they meet your terms.* For comparison, Win Your Money Back Offers (Attraction Offer #1) give customers the chance to get their money back *if they meet the terms.* In Trial With Penalty Offers, customers only pay *if they don't meet the terms.*

Ideally, the terms should be things that make excellent customers. So, they'll mirror the actions and results used in your Win Your Money Back Offer. But this time, we use *avoiding fees* (rather than winning money back) to incentivize adherence.

So Trial With Penalty isn't "here's my thing—see if you like it." It's *"here's my thing, you get it for free so long as you do this stuff…which makes you a perfect fit for my next offer. And if you don't, then you have to pay for it."*

To do a Trial With Penalty downsell, you must consider what they have to do to avoid the fee, and how you charge them. Normally, you get one chunk of people to buy your main offer. So, offer that first. And the rest, you'll get on this downsell. Let's say you normally close three of ten people on your Attraction Offer. And now you downsell *another* four on a Trial With Penalty. Then, after the trial finishes, upsell three of them. You go from three sales to six sales—*doubling* your customers! If you only have one offer, you lose everyone who says no. Downselling trials with a penalty gives people another chance to say yes.

I'm still irritated at the *thousands* of customers I've lost on free trials over the years before learning this. But now we can save them! The Trial With Penalty makes it happen.

Examples

Business to Consumer Offer: 28 Day Kick-That-Habit Blueprint

☐ To get the trial for free (and avoid the penalty fee), you must…

☐ Attend all your consulting calls

☐ Post your progress in the group once per week

☐ Journal daily in our app

☐ Attend feedback sessions and transformation sessions (aka—upsell opportunities)

Business To Business Offer: 5-Day Get Your First 5 Customers Challenge

☐ To get the trial for free (and avoid the penalty fee) you must…

☐ Send 100 outbound messages per day

☐ Report stats on outbound messages

☐ Attend the daily training

☐ Post in group daily once you've done homework

☐ Attend your graduation call (upsell opportunity)

Software: $500 Onboarding for HR Software, then $99 Per Month Thereafter

☐ Trial With Penalty: You don't have to pay $500 up front, but you must…

☐ Attend Onboarding, which is three, sixty-minute Zoom calls (upsell opportunities)

☐ Do the homework

☐ Activate your employer profile

☐ Get your employees set up by the end of the third call

Otherwise, you pay the fee.

Important Notes

What They Get For Free And What They Have To Do To Avoid The Fee. You'll need to know what your *terms of service* will be. The valuable parts will be either your bare bones offer (like the Decoy Offer) *or* your Win Your Money Back offer. Either work. I'd recommend giving more rather than giving less—if you can afford it. The criteria should activate and retain customers. You can swipe these directly from Win Your Money Back—Attraction Offer #1.

Breaking Up Fees vs. One Lump Fee. Say you have a $500 product with ten things to do. I'd rather bill $50 for each mess up than one $500 fee on their first mess up. On the other hand, if missing once really messes up their success, you'll want the fee to reflect that. I've seen both work.

How To Downsell The Trial. Here's a graphic to show how I downsell a Trial with Penalty in five steps.

Offer The Trial Last. If someone makes it clear they don't want your first offer, then downsell the Trial With Penalty. Here's how it might sound: *"Hmmm...that sure is a pickle. I'll tell ya what. How about we just get ya started for free, would you be okay with that? We can just help you out, and if you like it, you can stay. Let me get your ID and we can get the process started—fair enough?"*

Always Get A Credit Card. Record their info, hold onto the ID, and motion for their credit card saying. *"What card do you wanna use?"* <u>They have to leave a card</u>. If they balk, just say *"That's just how we've always done it."* If they still refuse, wish them a lovely day and show them out.

Pro Tip: If someone doesn't agree to put their card down *and* do the work, I won't sell them. They complain more and they convert less. Not worth the hassle.

Always Sell Staying And Paying. Ask <u>directly</u>: *"If this program got you the result, will you stay long-term?"* You want them to agree to staying long-term if you get them results. If they say no, there's no point in giving them a trial.

Then, we frame the conversation as if they'll stay long-term, even if we haven't started billing them yet. So if they say 'no,' but want more explanation, say something like this: *"I don't want you to try it. I want you to get results. And out of integrity, I want to set realistic goals. You are not going to hit your long-term goals during this trial. But, you will establish habits that will help you get there. And we're gonna help you do that for free. But if you wanna get to your long-term results, you're gonna have to stay on after. I just wanna make sure that you're not looking for a quick fix—because I can't ethically promise you that."*

Once they agree, move on.

④ EXPLAIN HOW FEES MOTIVATE

Explain the fees *after* getting their card. I say something like: *"We will do our part so long as you do yours. That's fair right? So now I just ask that you bet on yourself—if you miss or skip any stuff, your results will suffer. We charge to keep you on track. If you miss, no big deal. You'll get dinged a little fee but it'll get you back on track. If you follow through, you get all this for free. So this is the best way we can get you amazing results and keep it free for you. Best of both worlds."*

Note: If you explain the fees *before* you get the card, you will get more resistance. So explain *after* with a *'this is just how we've always done it'* attitude. People still have to agree to the fees, but you'll get a higher take rate doing it this way. I always have customers initial separately next to the fee clauses to force my sales guys to explain them.

⑤ MAKE SALES MEETINGS PART OF TRIAL

Make Check-ins Required. First, we explain *all* criteria so they understand the costs and benefits of adhering. Then, we draw attention to check-ins (our upsell opportunities): *"Yep, and you agree to attend each of the three check-ins. The first we do X so that you can [benefit one], the second we do Y so that you can [benefit two]…, the third we do Z so that you can [benefit three]… Obviously we charge if you miss these because it's the only way we can get you results."*

How I Upsell From A Trial. When someone takes a trial, one of three things happen: they like it, they hate it, or they don't use it. Here's how I upsell them from each scenario.

1) <u>If they like it:</u> This is the easy one. You already have them set up for automatic billing. Great! Meet with them anyway. You can still offer a longer term or higher value version of your service (or both). Successful customers tend to get even more value out of your better (and more profitable) stuff.

2) <u>If they hate it:</u> *Turn that frown upside down.* Ask them what they would have liked to be different. Tell them they're totally right, and that you're angry at yourself for missing this. *Do not blame them.* Only one person can be angry— and it needs to be you. Ask if they'll give you a chance to make it up because of how outraged you are at their experience. And now, since you better understand their needs, that they're a better fit for your higher level thing. Then, offer it to them. Yes—this is a sale. I can get about half of these people to buy.

3) <u>If they didn't use it.</u> *Reach out to people multiple times before you get to this point.* Explain that you need to meet with them. Offer to waive the fee if they do. Now, you can try to get them back on track or offer something better for them. I don't like billing non-starters. A small fee isn't worth a 1-star review. But hey, it's your choice.

Tweak Your Trial To Get The Most Customers. If no one takes your Trial, lower the requirements or penalties. If people take your Trial but don't follow through, emphasize explaining how fees help them and make sure you include sales meetings as mandatory. If people don't stay on the back end, better emphasize the value of staying and paying, get better at delivering, and make sure what you sell on the back end *makes sense* with what you sell on the front end. If you start printing money, don't stop.

Let People Make Up For Goofs. People often get discouraged after getting billed. But, you can offer an opportunity to 'make it up.' This does a great job of getting people back on track and converting. But, if they miss that, you're justified in billing them.

Just Call It A Trial. Even though the Trial With Penalty has some 'special features,' you should just call it a Free Trial. Otherwise, people may get scared and confused. No one wants to be penalized. And if they ask you why you do Free Trials this way just reply with *"This is just how we've always done it"* or *"People get the best results this way."*

Pay Less Now or Pay More Later vs. Trial With Penalty. I use Pay Less Now or Pay More Later as a downsell for physical products or one-time services. And I use Trial With Penalty as a downsell for recurring products or services. Also, I have only made this work in businesses where the customer has to do work to get results. If you find other types of businesses these work for…let me know!

Discounts Get Cards on File. Some people get weird when you offer free stuff and ask for a card. And if you have a super low price, it justifies asking for the card. The small price means the card will probably work when the automatic payments start. So instead of a free month, you might offer "first month for $1" then $X per month when it recurs.

Summary Points

- In a Trial With Penalty offer, customers can try your product or service for free *so long as they meet your terms.*

- Trial With Penalty downsell offers get yeses from people who've said no.

- To do them, you: get the card, get the commitment, explain what they have to do to get results and the meetings they must attend, and what happens if they don't.

- Trials With Penalties get more paying customers than normal free trials because they use your product more and actually get value from it.

- Use the same 'refund' criteria from Win Your Money Back (Attraction Offer #1) to create your Trial With Penalty criteria. This way, at the end of the trial, they've done the stuff that makes great long-term customers (and advertise your business for free).

- You can break fees up by criteria or you can charge a lump fee. I like breaking them up.

- You make money by getting people results and turning them into customers, not nickeling and diming people with fees.

- Use mid-trial check-ins to make more offers. If they love it, give them more of what they love. If they have problems with it, swap it for what makes sense for them. If they aren't using it, offer them the ability to make it up to avoid the fees.

FREE GIFT: Free Trial Training

Not all businesses can do free trials. But if you can, it's a helluva downsell. There's obviously right and wrong ways to do them and right and wrong businesses to do them in. I made a free video for you covering this chapter and as many details as I could. You can watch it at acquisition.com/training/money. I put a QR code for fast easy access.

Feature Downsells

Why don't we try this instead?

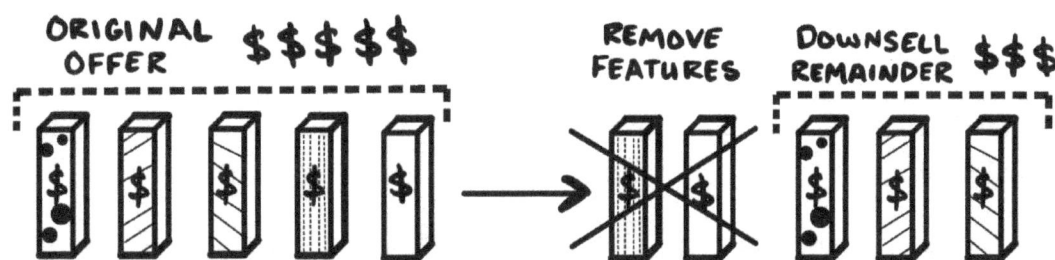

I can't remember when in 2019.

"This new downsell tripled my close rate from 25% to 75% last quarter. And even crazier, more people bought the main thing," he said between bites.

"You start offering a payment plan or a discount?"

"Neither. Payment plans take too long. And discounts devalue my product."

Huh… "We're talking about a high-ticket product, right?"

"Yup."

"Geez. What are you doing?"

"I lower the price, but I justify it by cutting a feature. That way, I'm not discounting."

"So what feature did you cut?"

"My full money-back guarantee."

"I never thought of guarantees as features, super intere–wait…*you downsell by removing your guarantee?*"

"Yea. Works great. When we get a price objection we ask '*If you don't want the option to get your money back, you can pay less. Or, you can keep your money-back guarantee—which would you prefer?*' Once they understand what they'd give up, they often say 'Screw it, I'd rather keep the guarantee and get my money back'."

"Ahhhh…so they only see the value of the guarantee *after* you remove it. And that also explains why so many more are buying the main thing. Clever." Then I followed up, "…how do the numbers break down?"

"Before, I only had one full-price option. So if 100 people got on a call, 25 bought. Now, 35 people buy the main thing and 40 take the downsell."

"So it upped your full-price buyers, total close rate, *and* up front cash. Nice!"

"Yeah, it changed my life," he said.

***

The last two chapters covered Payment Plan Downsells and Trial With Penalty. We downsold by keeping the overall price the same, only changing when and how they paid.

In this chapter, we cover Feature Downsells. With these, we downsell by lowering the price. But instead of a discount, which makes the same stuff cheaper, we lower the price *by changing what they get.*

Description

Feature Downsells lower prices by changing what customers get. I do them by offering lesser quantity, lower quality, lower price alternatives, or cutting optional components.

All features have a price and a value. If you remove something the price goes down, sure. But, the value goes down too. What features you remove and how much you lower the price affects how good of a deal the person gets. This change in your offer's price-to-value affects how people buy. People wanna get the *best deal for them.*

For instance, if you remove stuff they hate, and lower the price a lot, they get a *better deal.* If you remove stuff they love, and lower the price a little, they get a *worse deal.* Both get people to buy. In the story, customers loved the guarantee. *The guarantee had far more value than its price.* So even if they said no at first, removing the guarantee instantly showed its value. The customers saw the higher-price offer as *a better deal.* So, after seeing the downsell option, they bought the first offer.

People will see the value in the thing you removed *after they see the difference in price.* As in, people weigh how much money they save against how much value they lose. So, clever Feature Downselling gets customers to "re-upsell" themselves on the more expensive offers. This means you want to *remove features from highest to lowest value.* Since people want more value for their money, this incentivizes customers to make the highest value purchase for them.

Feature Downsells have a simple formula: take something away, lower the price, and in so many words ask "how about now?"

Feature Downsell Examples

Feature Downselling <u>Product and Service Quantity</u>. For services, this might mean a lower amount, fewer sessions, less time, or shorter duration. For products, it means fewer of them.

<u>Product Quantity Downsell</u>: *Instead of a three-month supply, how about we start with just one?*

<u>Service Quantity Downsell</u>: *Instead of four sessions per month, why don't we start you at two?*

Feature Downselling <u>Product Quality</u>. Think older versions, less reliable materials, materials of lower social status, etc.

<u>Product Quality Downsell</u>: *Instead of the leather seats we can do vinyl, how does that sound?*

Feature Downselling <u>Service Quality</u>. This means a lot of things. I will give you a few ways I change the quality of services. Hint: This also works to *increase* the service quality.

<u>Service Quality Downsell</u>: *Instead of 5-minute response times, why don't we just start you at overnight response times? You'll save some money and you'll still get your answers—just with a small delay.*

<u>More Service Quality Features</u>:

- <u>Time Availability</u>: Come specific times vs. whenever you want
  - o Days of week: Mon/Wed/Fri vs. All Days
  - o Times of day: 9 to 5 vs. 24hrs
  - o Amount of time: 15min Support Calls vs. 60min Support Calls
- <u>Location Availability</u>: This one location vs. all locations we own
- <u>Cancellations</u>: Reschedule fees vs. free
- <u>Speed Of Response</u>: Reply in minutes vs. hours vs. days etc.
- <u>Speed Of Delivery</u>: Wait in line vs. priority, same day/next day vs. next week etc.
- <u>Service Ratio</u>: One-on-one vs. one-to-many vs. many-to-one
- <u>Communication Method</u>: Text Support vs. Chat Support vs. Video Call Support etc.

- Provider Qualifications: Owner vs. long-time employee vs. new employee, etc.

- Live vs. Recorded: Watch it happening now vs. watch it *after* it happens later

- In-Person vs. Remote: Watch where it happens vs. watch it somewhere else

- DIY, DWY, DFY. Do It Yourself vs. Done With You vs. Done For You

- Expirations: Works forever vs. works for X time vs. works at specific times

- Personalization: Generic vs. made just for you

- Insurance/Guarantee:

    o Lengths of time: For One Year vs. For Life

    o Coverage: Specific bad thing happens vs. Any bad thing happens

    o Terms: Unconditional vs. Only if you do XYZ

Downselling by Removing Entire Features. Rather than lowering quantity or quality, you remove the feature itself. In the story, he removed a guarantee.

Removing Entire Feature Downsell: *Instead of priority chat support, email support, and calls, why don't we just keep chat and email support but drop the calls to save you some money? You'll still get your answers, it'll just save us time and we can pass those savings to you.*

Feature Downselling Done-For-You to Do-It-Yourself. If someone says no to all your service downsells, you can downsell another product that solves the same problem.

Done-For-You to Do-It-Yourself Product Downsell:

- Chiropractor: *Instead of chiropractic adjustments, let's start you with some tools you can use to do it yourself at home?* Then, you'd sell at home massage tools, foam rollers, mats, etc.

- Painter: *If you can't afford me painting your house, why don't I just give you the paint and let you lease one of our spray machines for a daily rate?*

- Alex Hormozi: *Instead of me and my team buying your company and actively growing your business, why don't you just attend a workshop?* (*Cough* Go to acquisition.com)

Important Notes

Remember, Never Negotiate The Price. People who demand to pay less for the same thing are business terrorists. I don't negotiate with terrorists. If they want to pay less now—offer a payment plan. If they want to pay less overall—offer a feature downsell. But don't let anyone pay less *just because.*

Maintain The Position Of A Helpful Guide. Remember, Feature Downselling means trying to find *the best deal for them.* This keeps the conversation collaborative rather than competitive. If you act pushy, your offers will exhaust customers faster. If you stay a helpful guide, you can downsell as many offers as necessary without exhausting the customer.

Tweak Your Feature Downsell Process. We have the job of making the product have the highest value-to-cost *in the eyes of the customer.* But, in the beginning, you won't know much about your customers' preferences. So, as you solve the same problems for the same type of customer, you'll learn what they find the most valuable. Once you do, you can standardize your Feature Downsell process. Feature Downsells close more people when you know what feature combinations to present ahead of time.

How I Standardize My Downsell Process. First, I cut something valuable and lower the price *a little.* I do this to get them to reconsider the original offer/price. If that fails, I continue removing features and lowering prices until they buy. I'd rather people get *something* rather than nothing.

Name Your Feature Combinations. Name the most expensive combination after a status your customer would find aspirational, such as "The Whale Package," "The Total Transformation," "High Roller" etc. Look at airlines. Make your version of First Class→Business Class→Economy.

I Name My Cheapest Combination "The Minimum." I like it because it implies they have to get *at least* that thing. If someone rejects all other packages, I just say "so nothing more than the minimum package then?" to get them to say no to say yes (like the Classic Upsell).

Temperature Check After Two Downsells (Like Payment Plans). If you make two changes in a row and they still refuse, make sure they really want the thing. I'd say something like *"Got it. Real quick. I want to make sure. On a scale from 1–10 how bad do you want this?"*

If They Say 8 Or Above, Start Payment Plan Downselling. *"Awesome. Don't worry. We're gonna figure out a way to make this happen for you."* If they say 7 or below, ask *"What would a 10 look like?"* and then, recombine the features to try and accommodate their '10.' Note: this means you can alternate between payment plan and feature downsells. When you use both, you become very difficult to refuse.

After Each Downsell, Ask "Deal?" Or "Fair Enough?" This works *astonishingly* well. Fewer people will see you change the offer for them and then say "No that's not fair." Listen to how I present Feature Downsells on Episode 202 of my podcast *The Game,* "How to close everyone: downselling like a pro."

Free Orientations Boost Do-It-Yourself Feature Downsells. Once someone has refused all my Done For You offers, I ask *"Even though we're not gonna work together on X, I still want to help. How about you just come to a free orientation on X tomorrow?"* At the end of the orientation, I offer a DIY product that solves the same problem as the DFY service. For example I offered a *free* orientation to people who refused my fitness offer. Of the people who showed up to the orientation (about half), almost all of them bought supplements. It got me money from people who would've otherwise said no. Free money for little extra work.

Feature Downsell Your Guarantees. If you already have a guarantee, make removing it part of your Feature Downsell process. People value security, so removing it gets many people to realize its value. This often flips an initial 'no' back to a 'yes.'

Feature Downsell Current Customers. Customers who use all the features they pay for keep paying longer than people who don't. So once you see a customer isn't using a feature, offer a lower price—only paying for the features they use. They'll either tell you they want to keep it and might start using it again—or—they'll be happy you gave them a *better deal.* It takes work, but it beats them canceling. Fun fact: Customers who we've downsold into a lower package *just for them* have the second highest value of all my customers. When people have a product they like at a price they find fair, they keep paying.

Barter With Reviews, Testimonials, And Referrals. Bartering is the oldest form of exchange. My sharp rock for your rabbit skin. And I love bartering. If I get a price objection, sometimes I offer discounts in exchange for advertising. Ex: *"I'll knock $100 off if you: 1) Leave me a review on all review sites 2) Leave me a video testimonial 3) Make a public social post at the beginning, middle, and end of our program showing your progress 4) Introduce me to two friends who you would want to do this with. Deal?"* To me, the advertising is worth more than the $100 discount. To them, the $100 is worth less than the advertising. Win-win.

Summary Points

- Feature Downsells lower prices by removing stuff.

- You take something away, lower the price, and ask "how about now?"

- Typical Feature Downsells offer Lesser Quantity, Lower Quality, Lower Price Alternatives, or remove features altogether.

- People tend to see the value in what you removed *after they see the price difference.* This may get more people to take the more expensive offer.

- If you remove stuff they hate, and lower the price a lot, more people take the downsell.

- If you remove stuff they love, and lower the price a little, more people take the original offer.

- The first downsell gets them to *reconsider my first offer.* The rest of my downsells get them to consider *the best deal for them.*

- If a prospect rejects multiple downsells, see if they still want your thing before continuing.

- If a prospect likes a combination of features, but still doesn't like the price, start payment plan downselling. Very effective.

- Feature downsell current customers *before* they cancel.

- You can discount customers in exchange for them advertising your business.

FREE GIFT: Feature Downsell Training [No Opt-in]

Understanding features within services and products gives you a huge advantage. It can help you make your stuff super profitable *while* staying attractive to the customer. This is one of my favorite topics and I made you an additional training that covers it. You can watch it, as always, at acquisition.com/training/money. I put a QR code for fast easy access.

Downsell Offers Conclusion

Everybody buys something.

Downsells give you another shot at getting a customer by turning *nos* into *yeses*. For that reason, it's less about having a hundred different products with the same offer, and more about having a hundred different offers for the same product. But, no matter what, the offer is *never the same stuff for cheaper.* We just keep tweaking the offer until we make it *the best deal for them.* The extra cash explodes our 30-day profits and blows us past our goals.

So we've used attraction offers to get customers to *buy once.* We've used upsells to get them to buy the next thing. And now I've shown you my three most powerful downsell processes *in case they say no*: Payment Plan Downsells, Trial With Penalty, and Feature Downsells.

Next, we've got the final stage of a *$100M Money Model*—Continuity Offers: *how to keep them buying for good.*

SECTION V:
CONTINUITY OFFERS

You can shear a sheep for a lifetime, but you can only skin it once. - John, an early mentor

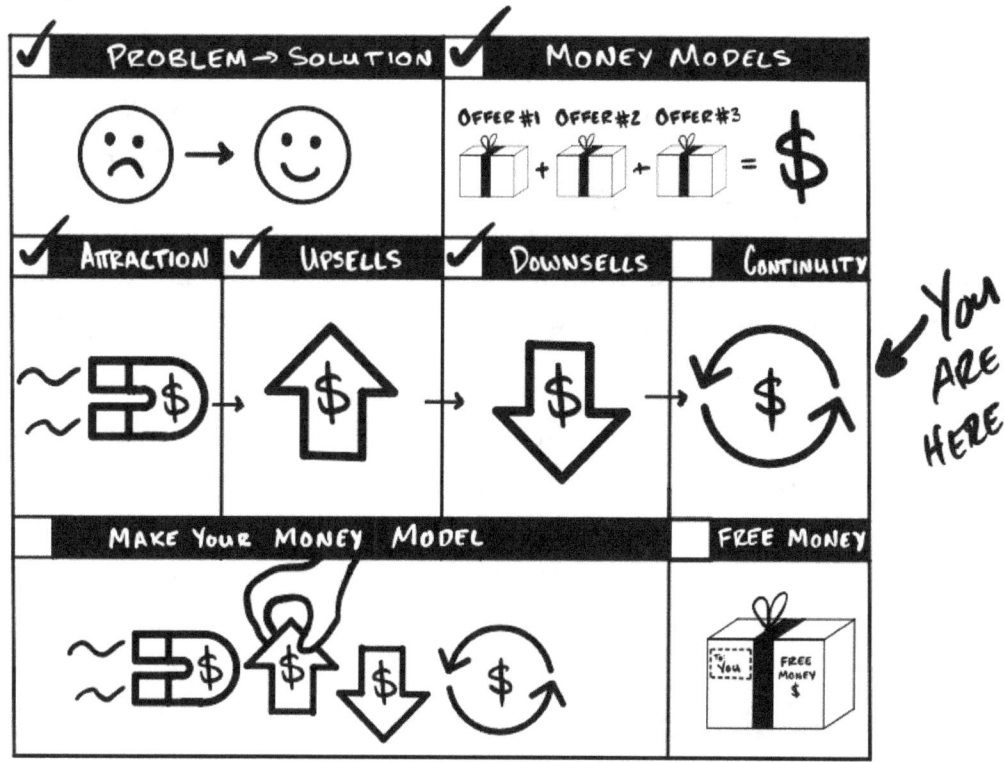

I've been a continuity guy my entire life: personal fitness, then gyms, then gym licensing, then supplements, then software, and now with Acquisition.com…lots of stuff. Needless to say, I'm a fan. Main reason: when you do continuity right, you get more customers *and* make more money from them. Continuity Offers *provide ongoing value that customers make ongoing payments for—until they cancel.* They boost the profit from every customer and give you one last thing to sell. Continuity Offers are awesome because you sell once, but get paid again and again.

Let me explain.

Let's say you offer a $1,000 thing to 100 people and 10 buy—you make $10,000 (10 x $1,000).

Now, let's say you talk to the same 100 people but you make your $1,000 thing…$50 per month instead. At fifty bucks, we can get 40 out of 100 to buy. And, if you keep those people for twenty months. *You still make $1,000 from each customer.* You go from making $10,000 now and $0 over time to $2,000 now and $40,000 over time.

As an added bonus, in the first example, if you only sold 10 customers, you'd only have 10 customers to upsell later. If you used a Continuity Offer and sold 40 customers, <u>you'd have four times the customers to upsell later</u>. A massive difference.

This illustrates the pros and cons of continuity. You can attract more customers compared to something more expensive, but you make *way* less money *now*. That makes it tough to use as an Attraction Offer *on its own*. Even if you have more money-making potential tomorrow, Continuity Attraction Offers leave you strapped for cash today.

By making continuity offers *last,* we get the best of all worlds. We get cash today from Attraction Offers, Upsell Offers, and Downsell Offers. We get a little cash today and tons of cash tomorrow from Continuity Offers.

To be clear—you can make Continuity Offers wherever and however you want. They can attract new customers, upsell and downsell current customers, or re-engage old customers.

Also, only *some* stuff makes sense for a Continuity Offer. It's silly for someone to pay for a one-day workshop…forever. It makes sense for them to pay until they cover the cost— and that makes it a payment plan. At the same time, you probably make a mistake to offer a single price (even a big price) to provide a service forever. If your customers get ongoing value, it probably makes sense for them to make ongoing payments.

The Three Continuity Offers

All offers depend on getting customers to buy. But, Continuity Offers depend on getting customers to keep buying. I get them to do both by combining bonuses, discounts, and fees.

- Continuity: Bonus Offers

- Continuity: Discount Offers

- Waived Fee Offer

Now that we got that covered. You can't get customers to stick to your continuity offer unless they've started…so let's start there.

FREE GIFT: Continuity and Continuity Offers Training

Almost every business I've built has been driven by continuity. It's a snowball that grows and grows. I made a video for you that outlines more training on the topic. You can watch it free (without giving your email) at acquisition.com/training/money. Scan the QR code.

SCAN ME

Continuity Bonus Offers

If you like this, you're gonna love what I have next...

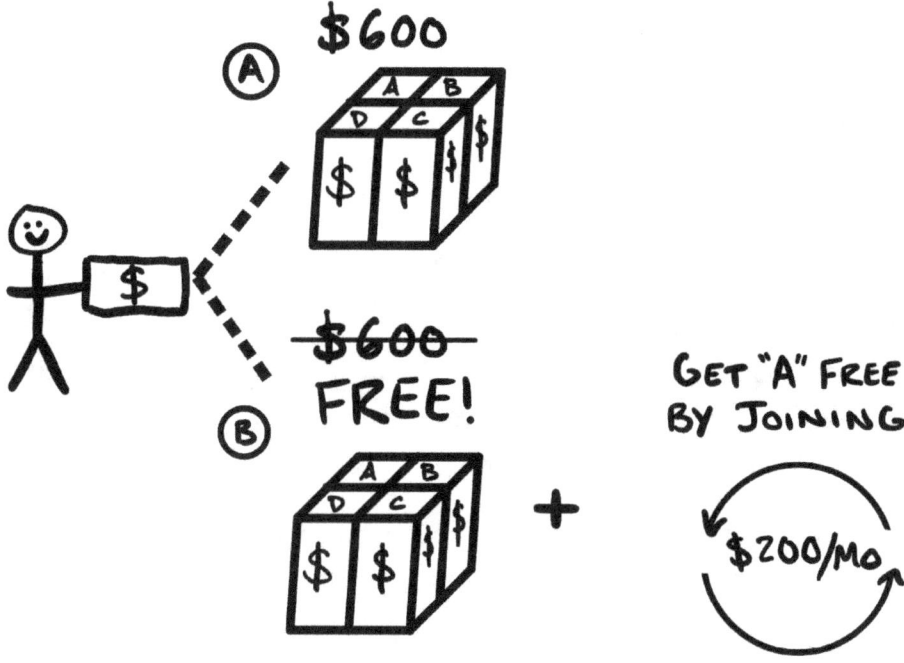

Fall 2019. When I learned that bonuses got more people to join continuity programs...

I taught gym owners how to sell six-week challenges and they were making money hand over fist. But some of them weren't that good at converting people into continuity after the challenge. Then, out of the blue...I saw a gym that used to struggle posting numbers *way higher* than some of our best performers.

Naturally, I investigated...

"Dude—your numbers are insane. How do you convert so many members?" I asked.

"I'm not really doing the six-week challenge," he said.

"Wait. What do you mean? You're marketing the six-week challenge though, right?"

"Yep. But I offer them something else when they come in."

"Okay...help me understand."

"So we go through the normal pitch. We explain the price. Yada yada. As soon as they say they're interested, we ask if they want to get it for free. They of course say yes. Then, I tell them that if they become a member, we'll make it free, which they love. And on top of that, if they become members, *they also get* member-exclusive bonuses. Members get better class times, the tanning booth, VIP events, all sorts of cool stuff. It converts like crazy. Last, we upsell a discounted prepaid membership."

"How does that go?" I asked.

"Well, for anyone who joins, we immediately ask '*wanna save even more money?*' They lean in. Then we offer a prepaid discount and bonuses for six months of membership."

"This is awesome. Does anyone even take the original challenge offer anymore?"

"Some do, sure. Can't be mad at more up front cash."

"I dig it. Break down some of your numbers, would you?"

"Before, we'd get thirty-four out of a hundred to sign up for the challenge. Then, a few weeks later we'd convert half (*seventeen*) to stay. Now, we only get like fifteen to sign up for the challenge but we get *forty* to go straight into continuity. And of those forty, about eight of them take the six month prepayment upsell."

"So let me get this straight…you *tripled* membership sales…you *still* get up front cash from challenges…*and* you stack even more up front cash from prepaid memberships??"

He could barely contain his grin. And for good reason. His tiny tweak was genius.

Description

With Continuity Bonuses you give the customer an awesome thing *if* they sign up today. Typically, the bonus itself has more value than the first continuity payment. That's all there is to it.

Bonus—adding value. For products, you can give away many small things or one big product that complements the subscription. For services, you give away a defined program, onboarding, setup, or feature that adds value.

Discount—lowering costs. Remember, anything you offer for free you can also offer as a discount. Free stuff and discounts both affect how we make decisions. So, we want to do *both* to get the benefits of both.

When making Continuity Offers, I get more people to *start* if I add more good stuff (bonuses) and take away bad stuff (discounts). And of course, it all works better with a dash of urgency—if they join *now*. Also, you can offer the bonus as a standalone purchase, or you can *only* make it available if they buy your continuity. Either works.

On their own, Continuity Offers get less cash now, and that makes it tough for getting customers profitably. But the way I use them, we can still hit our 30-day profit goals. Here's how: First, I do all my big-cash Attraction, Upsell, and Downsell offers. Then, Continuity Offers get a little bit of cash from the first month's payments. Then, I offer people who bought one month a discount on prepaying more months. This further boosts 30-day profits, giving me more cash to advertise, *and* stacks recurring revenue. Not too shabby.

Author Note: No successful continuity businesses I've seen has a standalone membership offer. They all have other bells and whistles to upsell. Main reason: Continuity Offers are tough to advertise profitably. Nobody wants to make a recurring commitment to something they haven't tried. To make up for this, businesses attract customers with stuff like trials. Then, once people join, they upsell other features and longer-term prepay options. This gets them the cash they need to advertise *while* building their recurring revenue.

Examples Of Getting People To Start On Continuity

Physical Product: Pet Food Continuity Offer

One-Time Bonus: Get every dog toy we've ever made for free, an $800 value, when you sign up for monthly dog food shipments for $59 per month.

Monthly Bonuses: You'll get a new dog toy every month as a member.

Service: Short-Term Accelerator Offer

One-Time Bonus: Short-Term Accelerator costs $1,000 on its own. Get it free when you become a member for $100 per month.

Bonus Package: The VIP community members enjoy first in line access to our events, longer support hours, better support reps, etc.

<u>Digital Product Offer</u>

One-Time Bonus: Get all my past 40 newsletters valued at $15,880 by becoming a member today for only $399/mo after a 30-day free trial.

Lifetime Discount + Lifetime Bonuses: If you pay today, you can lock in a lifetime discount to $299 per month. Get early digital access *and* a physical copy every month.

Note: Use the elements from the Feature Downsell chapter to create better bonuses.

Important Notes

Focus On The Bonus, Not The Membership. "Join my membership program" isn't nearly as compelling as "get this free valuable thing." So advertise that. Then, explain the rest after they show interest.

Bonuses Work Kinda Like Upsells.

More of the same: You get two years of past newsletters free by becoming a member.

Complementary: You get nutrition services for free when you sign up for our fitness membership.

Upgrade: You get a free gold membership when you buy a bronze membership (limited availability).

Keep Your Bonuses Related To Your Core Offer. If the bonus is too different you will *attract the wrong customers.* For instance, don't advertise a free t-shirt to upsell tech services. But, advertising a free t-shirt to upsell t-shirt printing makes sense.

Make Bonuses Things You <u>Already</u> Have And Do. For instance, the two past years of newsletters cost no extra time but are super high value. And onboarding is something you have to do with the client anyways, so you might as well slap a price on it and give to 'em as a bonus. If you value it, they will too.

Physical Bonuses on Digital Products and Digital Bonuses with Physical Products. If I have a digital membership, I might offer a hat, shirt, or tool, etc. related to the offer. If I have a physical product or service, like a boxing gym membership, offering live stream classes can get more people to sign up. This strategy often lowers the cost of getting a customer more than the cost of the bonus. And that's the point. Also, if some people take the bonus and run, the lower advertising costs can still make up for it. If customers are too expensive, give it a try.

Use Realistic Bonus Pricing. The bigger the value-anchor on your bonus, the more compelling the offer. But, you also have to make that anchor believable. Some business owners make up ridiculous values. Don't do this. It won't anchor the customer and you'll lose trust with them. This is a great opportunity to give away products you've sold before. You can anchor their actual prices as *real* discounts and bonuses.

You Can Bonus Your Customers By Giving Them Titles. Consider giving customers titles after they stay three, six, or twelve months and beyond. Titles like silver, gold, diamond, double diamond, etc. A good friend of mine does this, and after a while, she found her customers cared more about the title than any other bonus. She told me they even introduced themselves to her by their title! So, if you can't think of something to give them, at the very least, you can call them something special.

You Can Make Free Bonuses Discounts and Make Discounts Free Bonuses. Free Bonus: Become a member for $200 then you get this $1,000 program as a free bonus! Steep Discount: Get the $1,000 program for $1 if you become a member for $200.

When Making Your Continuity Offer, Anchor The Bonuses. First, sell them the benefits of the amazing bonus. Not your Continuity Offer—the bonus. Then, <u>use your high-value bonus as an anchor.</u> It may shock them—and *that's okay.* Because then you ask, "Do you want to know how you can get this for free?" If they do, which they will, explain how: *"Become a VIP member today and you'll get it all as a free gift for joining. Or, you can just buy it for $XXX—which would you prefer?"*

More Bonuses Get More People To Join. After you ask them if they want to know how to get it for free, you tell them they can get it when they join. <u>Then you say</u> *"on top of that...*when you become a member you'll get...amazing thing 1, amazing thing 2, amazing thing 3." *Mention the individual dollar values of each to anchor the value.* Stacking bonuses this way gets even more people to join your continuity.

Making Bonuses Available Only To Those Who Join. If you want to force everyone into continuity, then offer continuity as the only option. In other words, make the bonuses *only available* if they join the membership.

Pricing For Continuity vs. Up Front Cash. For whatever reason, some people pick one-time payments over continuity...*even with higher one-time payments.* So offer a higher one-time payment option. This way some customers will make you more money *today* while others stack recurring revenue for *tomorrow.* We change the price depending on our goals. I've tested this a ton and, at least for me, the data in this range look clear. Check it out:

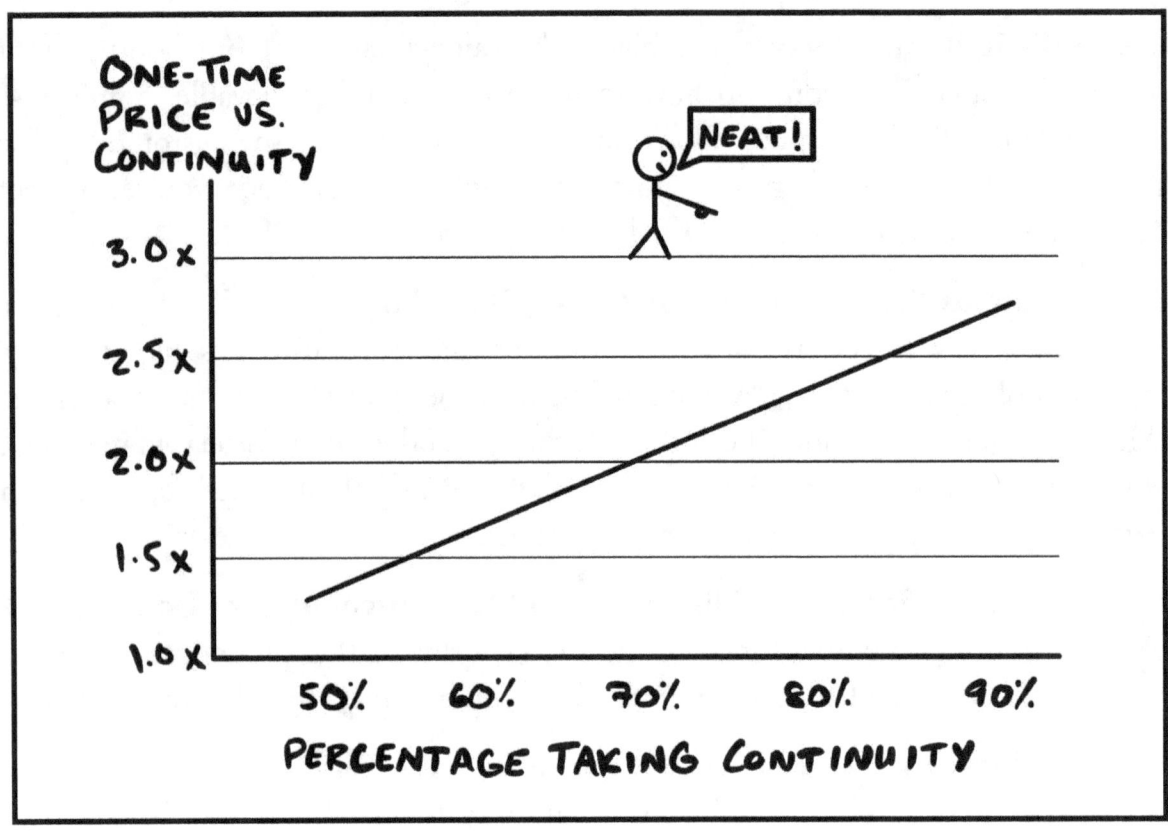

To get 50% to choose continuity make the standalone offer 1.33x more.

Ex: $399 standalone ($266/mo) or $199/mo membership

To get 60% to choose continuity make the standalone offer 1.66x more.

Ex: $499 standalone ($333/mo) or $199/mo membership

To get 70% to choose continuity make the standalone offer 2x more.

Ex: $599 standalone ($399/mo) or $199/mo membership

To get 80% to choose continuity make the standalone offer 2.33x more.

Ex: $699 standalone ($466/mo) or $199/mo membership

To get 90% to choose continuity make the standalone offer 2.66x more.

Ex: $799 standalone ($532/mo) or $199/mo membership

The exact numbers matter less than the principle. *The smaller the standalone price compared to the continuity price, the more people buy the standalone. The larger the standalone price compared to the continuity price, the more people choose continuity.*

142

If You Want More Up Front Cash. Make bonuses and continuity+bonuses *separate* offers. Make the bonus-only offer a single payment that's 1.33x to 2.66x more expensive than the first month of the continuity+bonus offer. The bigger the price difference, the fewer standalone purchases you'll have. But, the more money you make up front from each. Based on the data I just shared, people pay 33% more to *avoid* continuity. In other words, even if you charge 33% more for a one-time purchase, half will buy it!

If You Want Even More Cash—Offer Bulk Prepaid Discounts. Bulk continuity upsells boost 30-day profits by a lot. Let's say you offer "buy five months get one free." Only *one out of every eight people* has to take the upsell to raise 30-day profits by 50%! That can make or break your Money Model. Note: The laws of discounting apply—the larger the discount, the more people will take it.

If You Want Commitments—Prepare To Make A Trade. If you want commitments, trade them for bonuses. For example, only allow customers to get the bonus if they commit to 3-6-12+ months. When you only give it to customers who commit, you'll lose people who would've signed up month-to-month just to get the bonus. This nets fewer sales, but more committed customers. This is the trade you make.

Summary Points

When it comes down to it, offering real discounts and then following up with valuable free bonuses *makes people excited* about your offer. Then, if they agree to your continuity offer, you can further upsell blocks of time to boost your 30-day profits even more.

- With Continuity Bonuses you give the customer an awesome thing *if* they sign up today. Typically, the bonus itself has more value than the first continuity payment.

- If you use Continuity as an attraction offer, advertise what you give away, *not* what you sell.

- Make your bonus related to your core offer so you engage the right leads.

- If possible, make your bonuses stuff you already have and do. This way, you don't need to change your business or create new products.

- More people start continuity if you add more bonuses and discounts.

- To add bonuses—add more good stuff *only* if they sign up.

- To discount—take away the cost of actual products, services, and features you sell.

- Sell the value of the bonus *before* telling them how they can get it for free.

- Offer bonuses as a standalone option for more up front cash.

- If you want half the people to take the standalone offer, price it 33% above your continuity.

- Boost up front cash even more by offering continuity at a discount if they buy in bulk.

FREE GIFT: Continuity Bonus Offers Training

There are so many insane ways to structure bonuses to drive more continuity sales. I made a video for you that covers this chapter and other creative ways I've seen them used. You can watch it free at acquisition.com/training/money. Scan the QR code for fast and easy access.

SCAN ME

Continuity Discount Offers

If you sign up today, you get X time free.

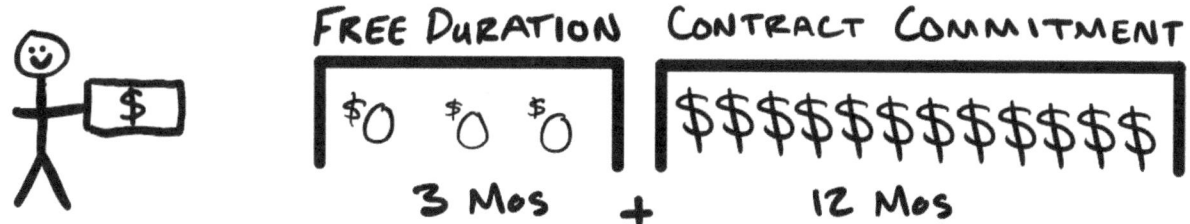

Spring 2018.

Leila and I had just moved into one of the nicer Austin suburbs. On our afternoon walk, a neighbor smiled and waved us over. It looked like she wanted to make "welcome to the neighborhood" small talk. *I hate small talk.* But as I got closer, I got more interested. The yard was perfect. A Ferrari stuck out of their garage for "spring cleaning." The patio table was littered with cigarettes and beer cans. *Huh?*

"Hi there, welcome to the neighborhood…let me get the husband." I smiled through gritted teeth. *Here we go.* Out came the character—in a backwards hat, flip flops, with a strong midwest accent, speaking a mile in a minute, and the widest grin you've ever seen.

"Hey brotherman! Nice to meetcha. I can tell yer no doctor or lawyer livin' here so young. So what kinda hustle you got?" He also got straight to the point. *Relief.*

I told him a bit about my gyms, launching gyms, and the rise of Gym Launch. He nodded with approval. He said he liked having another business owner on the street.

"What about you?" I asked.

He smirked. "*Trash.*"

"What?"

"*Trash.*"

He saw my confused look and continued.

"Alright, so ya see, I knew from my time workin' trash there wasn't much competition. Big commercial places and all went to the same place for their trash needs."

"So what did you do?"

"Well, I had a truck, took my credit card, and I gambled." He continued. "I went to all the big apartments and said I'd do their trash for a whole year free if they contracted me to do the next five years paid. It worked good enough. They all made me their trash man before I knew it."

"Dang," I said. "You fronted an entire year?"

"Uh-huh. And I'll tell you what, *it was the toughest thing I ever did*. No one would invest in my business, not even my family. They all called me crazy. But after that one year mark passed, the cash came floodin'. I ate *real fat* then. And after a few years usin' that plan, I sold the whole shebang for a pretty penny."

"Nice, man. I never would've thought there was so much money in trash."

"There's cash in trash baby, what can I say. Oh yeah…you want a beer, or what?"

Needless to say, we've stayed friends to this day.

***

Listening to his success showed me the sheer power of a simple offer done right. That said, let's go over some important stuff so you can make it work like he did.

Also, if you think this looks like "Buy X Get Y Free" done continuity-style, then you'd be right. However, there are enough differences specific to continuity that it justified its own chapter.

Description

To make a one-time continuity discount, you give products or services away for free if the customer commits to buying more products and services *over time*. This can attract loads of potential customers and makes an easy sale anyone can close.

If you look around, you'll see this offer in many different industries. It works. Think internet, pool cleaning, gym memberships, landscaping, and anything rentable. I mention common ones, but you can make this work in any business so long as you know two things. First, how you'll apply the discount—I do it four ways. And second, your cancellation policy—because people don't always keep their commitments.

Examples

I discount in <u>four</u> ways: Up front, at the end, an even spread, or after the first month or two.

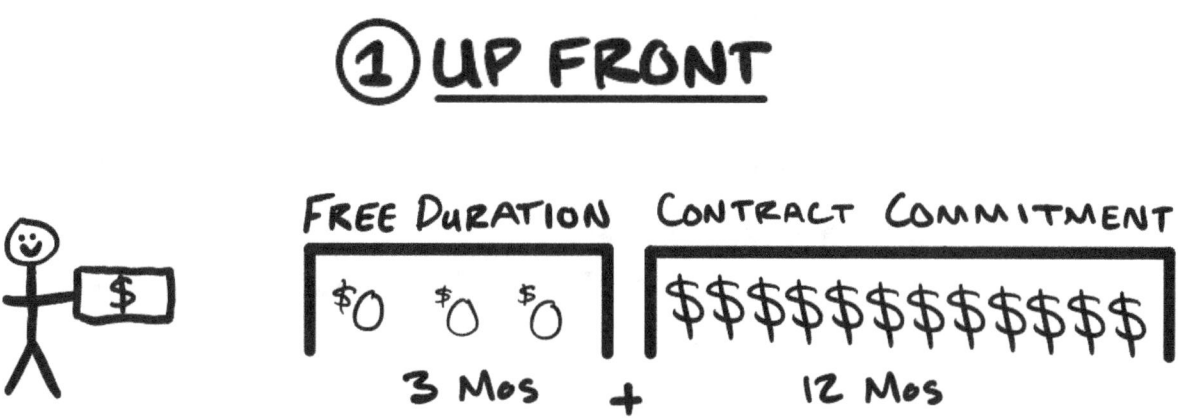

Up Front. You apply the discount up front and push out the term. As in, the "official" time starts after their free time ends. This works best in industries that have a successful history of enforcing contracts (cell phones, storage, real estate, equipment, or anything with collateral). Two notes: First, if you have historically high churn, then skip this one and consider the others. Second, this does <u>not</u> get customers profitably. It gets customers, but delays cash. So if you want more profitable options, continue on.

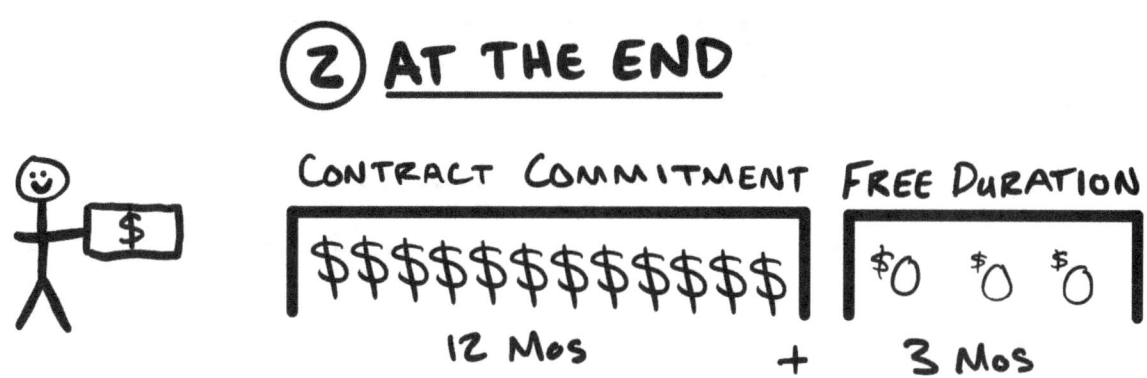

At The End. You can apply the entire discount at the end and push out the term. So long as they make every payment *on time*…they get a bonus time equal to the value of the discount. They *earn* their free time.

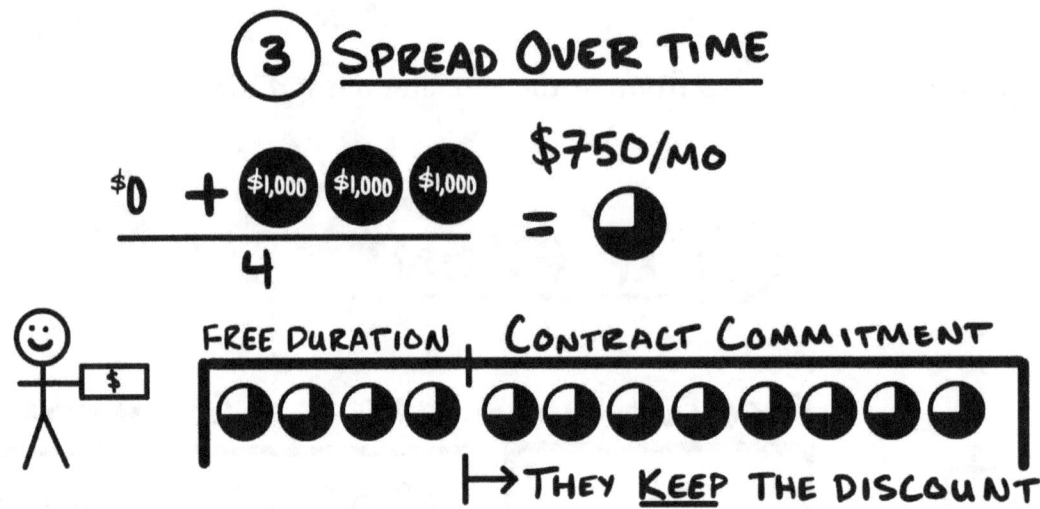

Spread Over Time. Apply the discount across the term. Say you give three months free for a one-year commitment. At $200 per month you've discounted $600. By spreading that $600 over 12 months, they get a $600/12 months = $50 discount *each month*. You can also tell them that if they make all their payments on time, they can keep the discount for life after the term is over.

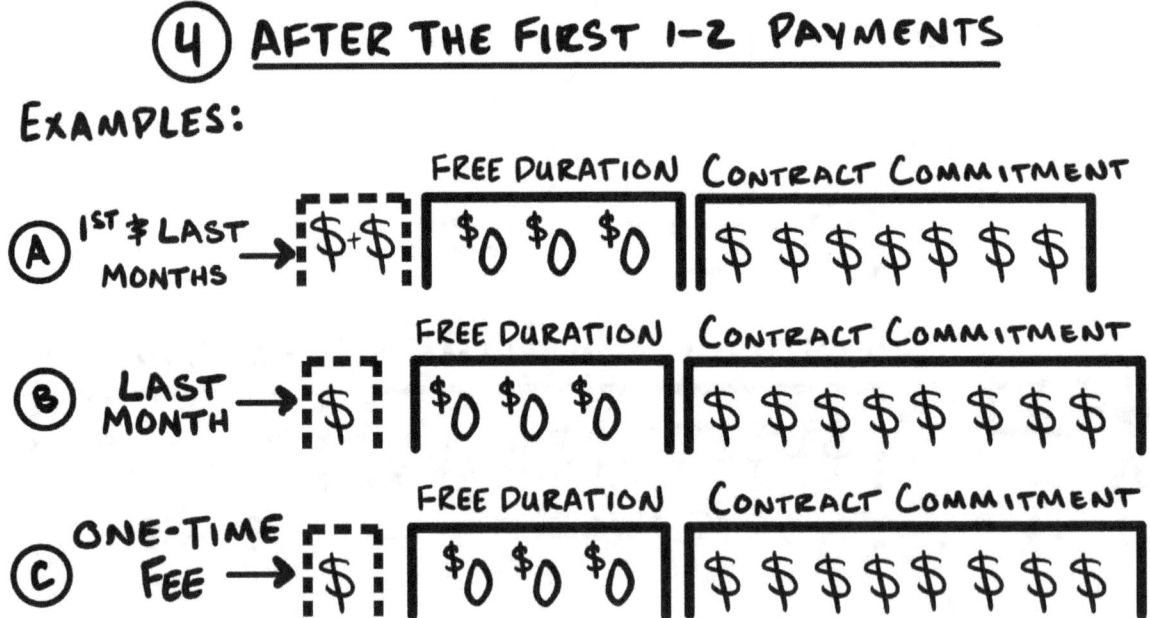

After the first 1–2 payments. They pay a few times and then they get their one-time discount. This way you collect a bit of cash to cover advertising and some delivery costs. I prefer to do it by presenting the offer as *"first and last month," "last month up front,"* or adding some sort of *activation fee* before getting the bonus value. It also ensures the customer uses a valid form of payment…a small but important detail when you run a business.

Important Notes

Highest Value Per Word Note In This Book <u>Skip this if you hate money.</u> Bill *weekly* (weekly, every 2 weeks, 4 weeks, 12 weeks etc). Here's why. There are 12 months in a year, but the year has <u>13</u> four-week cycles. *That's an 8.3% difference.* If I offer my thing at "$100 every four weeks" (versus $100 a month) the same number of people buy. But, I make 8.3% more annually. To put this into perspective, if your business has 20% margins, this skyrockets annual profit by 41%. And the best part is, you don't do any more work. Just change a few words. What else can you do legally that makes so much money for so little work? This has literally made me *millions in pure profit.* So yeah, do it.

Don't Eat Into The Term With Discounts, Extend Them! Let's say you offer three months free when you sign up for a year. That could mean they pay for nine months then get three free (12 total months). Or, that could mean they pay 12 months and get three free (15 total months). <u>I prefer to start with extending the term. Then, I can Feature Downsell a shorter one.</u>

Get 3% More Revenue For Five Extra Words. "Yea, it's $X *plus a 3% processing fee.*" In my life, I've never had anyone not buy because of a processing fee. But 3% added to your topline *for no extra work* goes straight to your bottom line. If you run a 10% profit business, and add 3%, you just added 30% to your profit. Worth it. And this works especially well when paired with…

Get Two Forms Of Payment. Recurring businesses lose mountains of cash because of payment processing problems. First, customers don't cancel but their payment information changes or expires. Second, customers max out cards or have insufficient funds. We fix both issues with the same solution. I ask them if they want a 3% discount (a pretty standard processing fee). *"Do you want to save the processing fee? …awesome. Give us a second form of payment in case anything happens to the first one."* If they ask why, which they rarely do, just say *"We only have the processing fee because it costs us man hours to get new payment information every month from our customers. So if you save us time, we pass the savings onto you."*

Get ACH If You Can. If you get a second form of payment, try to get ACH. This is a form of payment that links directly to their bank account. It's the cheapest way to transact besides cash. If you don't know what ACH is, look it up.

Gift Cards. Give the discounted time in the form of a physical gift card. You can mail it to them if they are out of the area. The customer can apply the discount whenever they want *after the first three payments or so.* Then you can say they can also gift it to a friend if they want. And now you've got a lead magnet! Beyond that, many people simply forget to use it. In that instance, you just got a full-priced sign-up. Nice!

Try Lifetime Discount At Your Most Common Churn Point. You advertise the lifetime discount. But, you make customers *earn* it. They get a lower rate *if* they stay past X period. Make X the month your average customer drops off.

Let's say you know every customer stays four months on average. You'd tell everyone <u>up front</u> they get a lifetime discount after month four. As the time approaches, tell them their new lower rate is right around the corner.

Real world example: I saw a rice company selling (a lot) of rice. They offered three pricing options: 1) a one-time price 2) a 5% off subscription 3) 15% off *if you stayed on the subscription for five straight months.* You earned the lifetime lower rate. I'm sure they figured out that it was just beyond where most people canceled.

CANCELLATIONS

You Need To Have A Cancellation Policy Figured Out Ahead Of Time. There are many common ones. 30 or 60 days notice. Cancellation fees. Cancel anytime. Etc. Since everyone comes into my Continuity Offers on a discount of some kind, this is my favorite:

Just make the cancellation fee *equal to the discount they agreed to get.* So if they got $600 in discounts by committing, they can pay $600 whenever they want to cancel. This is simple to explain.

Make Sure Customers Know How To Cancel. If customers have nowhere to complain inside your business, they will definitely complain *outside* of your business. If you have no obvious way for them to cancel, more people will vanish *and* complain. By having a clear way for them to contact you, then you can have a real chance to save it. *Small businesses don't get rich by making stuff hard for their customers.* If you make it easy, you'll suffer fewer 1-star reviews and have a chance to save them when they do—because you'll know about it.

If A Customer Wants To Cancel, Ask To Do An Exit Interview. Some people like to vent. Let them. Get more angry about the problem than them. They may try to calm you down. Sometimes, they will save themselves! If they complain about something you can solve then, by golly, solve it. And if they wanted a better product, do a rollover upsell into a higher level of service if you have one to offer. I've had many people buy a lower cost offer and then complain because they wanted the higher cost features. So I offer higher cost features, and they buy. Yes. It happens. And yes, it works.

Use Cancellation Fees To The Customer's Advantage. I might say "I'll waive your cancellation fee if you come in and tell me what I could do better." This gives customers a *real* reason to give feedback. Then, I can use their feedback to fix the problem—or—offer something better suited for them. At the very least, they'll have nicer things to say about the business if I actually try to solve the problem. I routinely save a third of customers that agree to exit interviews.

Summary Points

- Continuity Discount Offers give continuity time for free *if* the customer signs up today.

- Frontloaded discounts convert more customers, but may have higher churn.

- Backloading discounts converts fewer customers, but they lower churn.

- Spreading the discount keeps cash flowing while providing the full discount.

- Use gift cards to give the discount to new customers and allow them to gift it to a friend or use it on themselves at a later date. You get a full priced sign-up and a referral!

- Allow customers to earn a lifetime discount *at your month of greatest churn* to encourage customers to stick through it for a lifetime lower rate.

- Light cancellation terms get more people to sign up but more people leave. Harsher terms get fewer sign-ups but fewer leave. I prefer customers cancel by paying the discount they got with their commitment. This puts them back at the month-to-month rate.

- Make sure customers know how to cancel.

- If a customer wants to cancel, ask for an exit interview. Incentivize them by saying you'll waive the cancellation fee if they do. You'll often be able to save or upsell them from the conversation. At the very least, you understand what went wrong so you can get better.

FREE GIFT: Continuity Discount Offers Training

Like bonuses, discounts are only limited by your creativity. In this chapter I gave you the building blocks. I also made you a video covering some of the creative ways I've seen. As usual, you can watch it free at acquisition.com/training/money. Or, scan the QR code. Enjoy.

Waived Fee Offer

You can sign up month-to-month with a setup fee, or I'll waive it if you commit to a year.

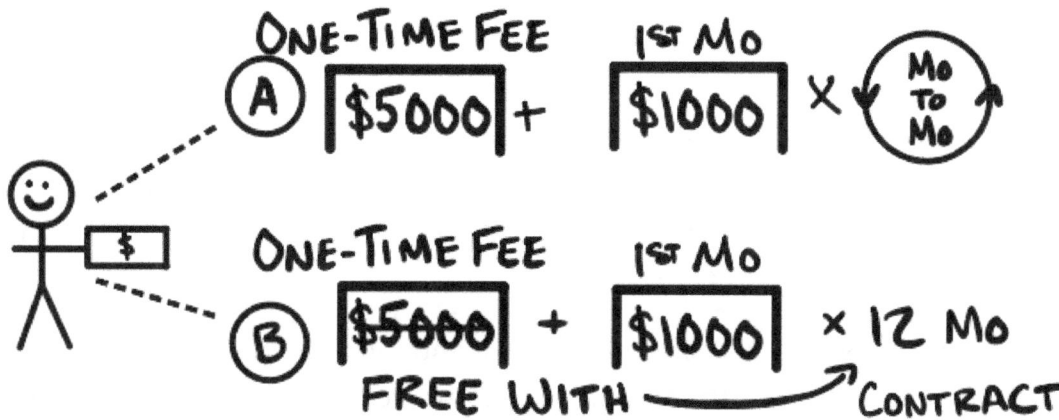

January 2021.

For years, I heard stories about this legend of high-ticket sales. Today, I finally got to meet him. But then, it got weird. You'd think a man with a reputation like his would also love working, but not him. In fact, his views about work nearly *opposed* mine—he aimed to *work as little as possible*. And those "lifestyle" guys tend to put me off. But he had his legendary reputation for a reason. So, it made me all the more interested…

"I'd rather make a few million bucks a year with zero employees and cool customers than build some gigantic business that panders to anyone willing to give me a buck," he said. "I don't need to feed my ego, I just collect monthly payments and chill."

Yeah right. "Monthly payments? That sounds less chill than up front. Don't you have to deal with churn, back outs, and all the other hassles of continuity?" I said.

"Nope. Not really. The way I sell is so simple you'll kick yourself once you hear it," he said.

"I'm all ears."

"I tell customers they have two options: *'You can go month-to-month with a big setup fee. It covers the cost of getting you started, but you can leave whenever. Or, if you commit to a year, I'll waive the fee.'* And I make the fee huge, so buyers commit to avoid it. I also have them initial that they understand they can quit early if they pay the fee I waived."

"Why such a big fee?" I asked.

"It costs a lot to quit in the beginning, so that keeps them engaged and—"

I chimed in "and once they pass that point, it costs about the same to cancel as it does to stick it out. So, they just stick it out."

"Bingo."

Description

Waived Fee Offers work like this. First, you ask the customer to pay a startup fee as part of joining a month-to-month program. Typically, I do 3–5x my monthly rate. Then, you offer to discount the *entire* fee *if* they commit longer term. But, if they cancel inside the term, they pay the fee.

Customers can choose to pay a significant fee and keep the option to quit at any time, or they can commit to 12 months and get the fee waived. Many will commit to avoid the big fee.

We take a greater risk if they pay month-to-month. But *they* take a greater risk if they commit. If a customer chooses month-to-month, we lower our risk with the startup fee. But, we lower *their* risk year-to-year by waiving those fees. And if they commit and want to quit early, then OK. They pay *as if* they had chosen "month-to-month" from the beginning. Simple.

Bottom Line: Customers will stay longer if leaving costs more than staying.

Example

Since the offer focuses more on pricing, it looks the same in all continuity businesses. The following example pulls from the story to give you a closer look at the mechanics.

Waived Fees With Commitment.

1) Commitment length - 12 months

2) Monthly rate - $1,000 per month

3) Fee - $5,000 *if they pay month-to-month*.

Option A: Pay a one-time fee of $5,000 *plus* $1,000 for the first month. Then pay $1,000 per month thereafter. Cancel whenever you want.

Option B: Waive the $5,000 if you commit to 12 months. Pay $1,000 per month. Only pay the $5,000 fee if you break your commitment early.

Important Notes

Fees Get Them To Start. People get value out of committing *immediately* because they avoid a fee. People want to avoid fees. So, more people sign up to continuity. Mission accomplished.

Fees Get Them To Stick. People will stick for the same reason they started. <u>By sticking, *they avoid the fee.*</u> People quit for millions of reasons. But, by incurring an additional and larger fee *in order to* cancel, their original reason for quitting immediately shrinks compared to the value of avoiding the fee. In English, if the cost to quit exceeds the cost to stay, they will probably stay.

Presenting The Fee. Justify the fee by explaining the costs of taking on new customers for long-term programs. Basically, if they want short-term flexibility, *they pay their own setup costs.* But, if they commit to staying long-term, *we pay their setup costs for them.* If someone asks for additional reasoning, just say: *"It costs us money to get you started. If you only wanna test us out, you cover those costs. If you commit longer, I'll cover them."*

If <u>More Than 5%</u> Of People Want To Cancel Early, Look Into It. Pricing *incentivizes* sticking but it can't (and *shouldn't*) overcome a terrible product. You want to nudge them, not handcuff people into paying for something they hate. Then, they'll just hate you.

If You Want More Up Front Cash, Have A Smaller Fee. A smaller fee encourages people to go month-to-month. A larger fee encourages people to make the commitment. But if you need more cash up front, you can make the fee 1.5–3x the monthly rate. When you do this, more people will take it, and you'll get more cash up front.

Drop The Fee After The Customer Fulfills The Commitment. If someone stays the entirety of their commitment, then wants to cancel, they have earned their free cancellation. It doesn't stick forever. This makes it equitable.

I Prefer This Offer For Commitments Of One Year And Longer. The longer the commitment, the better this works. It works especially well with services that take a long time to work (SEO, Investing, Weight Loss, etc.). It keeps people committed *when* they get emotional.

Cancellation Fees For A…Cause? If you want to keep customers extra motivated, you can donate it to a cause they are *against*. Ex: "What cause do you absolutely hate?…*Great. If you cancel early, I will be donating your setup fee to them.*" This gives them *two* reasons to stay. First, because they don't want to shell out the cash. Second, because they don't want a cause they hate to get it.

Summary Points

- Waived Fee Offers present a month-to-month option with a fee or waive the fee if they commit.

- I typically make the fee 3–5x my monthly rate.

- At minimum, the commitment length should be a year.

- The larger your fee, the more buyers will opt for the commitment. The smaller your fee, the more up front cash you'll get.

- If the customer meets the commitment, the fee officially goes away.

FREE GIFT: Waive Fee Video Training

Waived fees are so so so effective. I can't wait for you to actually use them and see for yourself. To make sure you feel confident doing them on your own, I made you a video walking you through them. As usual, you can watch it free at acquisition.com/training/money. Or, you can scan the QR code. Enjoy.

Continuity Offers Conclusion

The only thing better than getting someone to buy once, is getting them to buy again.

Continuity Offers *provide ongoing value that customers make ongoing payments for until they cancel.* Many businesses use Continuity Offers to attract customers for less. But, it crashes 30-day profits. This makes profitable advertising difficult.

I use Continuity Offers differently. I make them *last.* I start with profitable Attraction Offers. Then make my Upsell and Downsell Offers. *Then,* I offer Continuity. And if they accept, I upsell a bulk amount of time or product at a discount. Then, they automatically enter continuity after they've used up their bulk purchase. This way, I make even more cash *and* I get the recurring-cash benefits of the other continuity customers.

Continuity Offers work with rewards or punishment. I prefer rewards. And two of the three Continuity Offers I explained use them. But, there will always be times when a more traditional contract makes sense. In those situations, I like Waived Fee Offers.

In the next section we will create our $100M Money Model by combining all four offer types: Attraction Offers, Upsell Offers, Downsell Offers, and Continuity Offers. Let's put a bow on it.

SECTION VI: MAKE YOUR MONEY MODEL

How To Take Over Your Entire Market

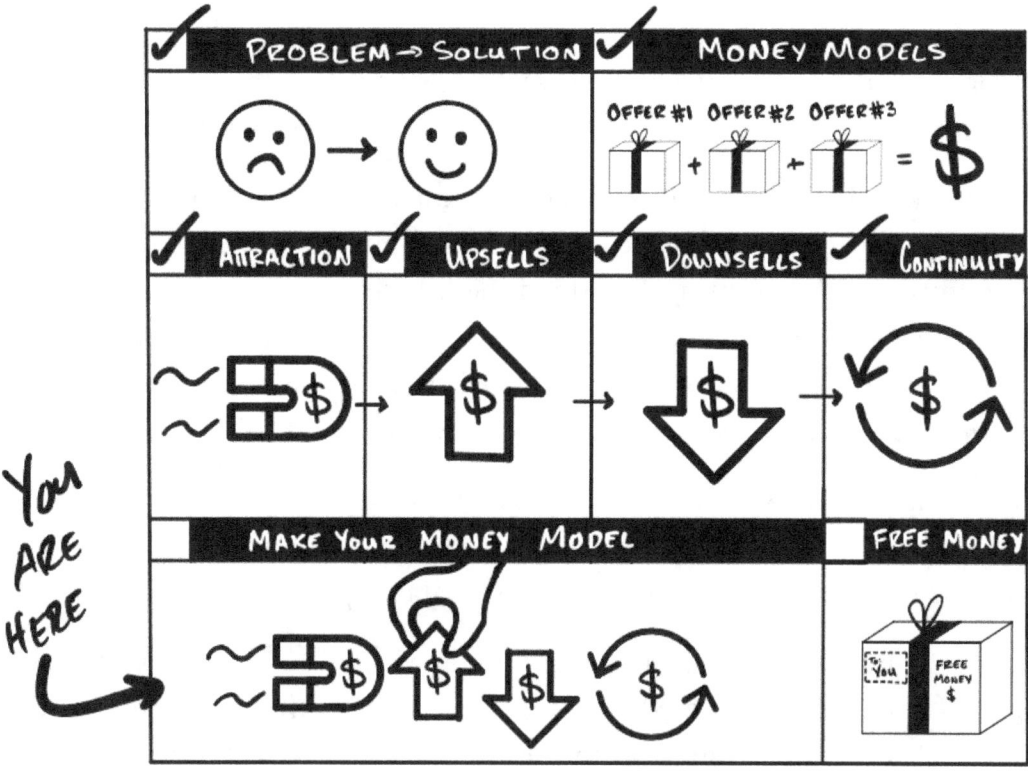

Looking back at the evolution of Gym Launch's $100M Money Model today.

I accidentally discovered the Gym Launch licensing Money Model. I went from flying around and filling gyms to licensing the stuff I used when I did it. This way, gym owners could do it themselves.

Looking back, it all started it with a <u>Decoy Offer.</u> I attracted new customers with lots of free courses, books, video training, live training, and so on. All stuff on growing a gym. Each free product came with its own free call to help gym owners use it. On the call I'd offer:

Decoy Offer: Now that you've got the plan, you do it on your own for free.

Or…

Premium Offer: We can help you implement all this stuff for $16,000 over 16 weeks.

If they took the premium option, they'd get a treasure trove of money-making tactics. Tactics that took me years to figure out. People bought left and right. *And whoosh, my Decoy Offer took me to $476,000 per month in three months. Not a typo.*

But I had a problem. Since I only had one thing to sell, I knew my revenue would plateau *fast*. I needed an upsell to raise profits or Gym Launch would stagnate. So I crafted an Upsell Offer for the more advanced gym owners. I called it "Gym Lords" and priced it at $42,000 per year. I used the Classic Upsell to offer advanced playbooks and services. And a community to share best practices as a Continuity Bonus. I started by offering a hefty *$6,000 discount* for anyone who prepaid. Many gym owners paid for it up front with money I had just made them. For the ones who didn't, I offered a Payment Plan Downsell.

If they said no, I went for $10,000 down and spread the rest over time. If they said no again, I'd go for ~$800 per week for 52 weeks. If they said no *again*, I said they could start for free. I'd use a Continuity Discount to frontload the free time for as long as it took them to finish paying off the first offer. Then, they'd roll right into my continuity upsell. This way, their payments stayed continuous. *And zoom…The Classic Upsell + Continuity Bonus + Payment Plan Downsell + Continuity Discount took me to ~$1,500,000 per month.*

I had another thing to sell. Woo! And it exploded Gym Launch's Money Model to the next level. But, I still had work to do. Even though the upsell and downsell process worked well, *some gym owners kept saying no.* I went back to the drawing board.

I came up with a more personalized Menu Upsell with different levels of service. I offered done-for-you advertising. I offered sales team training. I offered turnkey campaigns to make quick cash. And finally, I offered a minimum package—continuous access to the original Gym Launch materials *with tech support* for a discounted monthly rate. If they didn't want the whole package, I used Feature Downsells to find the best option for them. Almost everyone stayed for something.

And wham…Menu Upsells + Feature Downsells took me to $2,300,000 per month. All within 14 months.

Then we started Prestige Labs and integrated it with Gym Launch. A totally different business with its own Money Model. By month 20, we were raking in $4,400,000 *per month*. It was life-changing. And it *only* took a *few darn good products* and a *$100M Money Model* to do it.

***

Author Note: When I started, I didn't know any of this Money Model stuff. It only looks clean looking back. But, I hope this simplifies things so it takes you much less time than it took me.

Description

A Money Model is *a deliberate sequence of offers*. It's what you offer, when you offer, and how you offer it to make as much money as you can as fast as you can. Ideally, to make enough money from one customer to get and service *at least* two more customers *in less than 30 days*. And it rarely looks clean, but I break $100M Money Models into three stages:

Stage I: Get Cash—Attraction Offers get more customers for less

Stage II: Get More Cash—Upsell & Downsell Offers make more money from them faster

Stage III: Get The Most Cash—Continuity Offers maximize their total money spent

I break my $100M Money Model down into these stages because Money Model growth happens *alongside* the growth of the business. In other words, if you try to *start* a bootstrapped business, from zero, on your own, with a "finished" Money Model… it will collapse *on top of you*. In fact, *none* of my businesses started with a fully forged Money Model. They *all* start at Stage I. Even Acquisition.com! In my experience, Money Models evolve like this:

- First, I get customers reliably *then*

- I make sure they pay for themselves reliably *then*

- I make sure they pay for other customers reliably *then*

- I start maximizing each customer's long-term value *then*

- I spend as many advertising dollars as I can to print as much money as possible.

My Money Models develop this way because I make sure *each stage pays for the next*. We keep improving each stage until it gets *reliable*. Also, this means financial *and* operational reliability. So fair warning: when your Money Model starts working, your business starts *breaking*. Part of the game. So I suggest you find someone who can build and lead the team that makes your vision a reality. When I did, I married her. I hope the same luck finds you.

> **Author Note:** I want to make myself abundantly clear. *Lots* of *$100M Money Models* exist. I dare say a *$100M Money Model* exists for every $100M business! Remember, plenty of businesses make gobs of money in plenty of ways. I just show the ways *I have actually done it.*

Example Money Models

Gym Launch Money Model Breakdown (Services)

Stage I Attraction Offer: Decoy Offer

Free Do-It-Yourself Decoy vs. Premium $16,000 Done-With-You Licensing

Stage II Upsell Offer: Classic Upsell

Once you know how to get 'em, you gotta know how to keep 'em.

$42,000 Per year ($36,000 Prepaid) for advanced business services.

Stage II Downsell Offer: Payment Plan Downsell

Seesaw Downsell: *Start at $10,000 down with the rest spread over 52 weeks.*

Final Payment Plan Offer: *$800 per week for 52 weeks.*

Stage III Continuity Offer: Menu Close + Feature Downsell

Full Package: $800 per week

Feature: Done-For-You Advertising: $300 per week

Feature: Gym Sales Daily Training: $200 per week

Feature: Monthly New Releases: $500 per week

Feature: Original Licensing Materials with tech support: $100 per week

Minimum Package: $100 per week

Micro Gyms Money Model Breakdown (Local Business)

Stage I Attraction Offer: Win Your Money Back

> *Pay-to-enter fitness challenge. Win money back if you meet goals.*

Stage I Downsell Offer: Payment Plan Downsell

> Split Pay→ Three-Pay→ Free Trial With Penalty

Stage II Upsell Offer: Menu Upsell

> *You're not gonna get <u>the best</u> results without the right supplements.*

> Supplement Bundles: Big Bundle personalized to goal

Stage II Downsell Offer: Feature Downsell

> Supplements: Big Bundle→ Small Bundle→ Monthly Subscription

Stage III Continuity Offer: Rollover Upsell + Lifetime Discount

> $50 off per month for life with a 12-month commitment

Newsletter (Digital Product)

Stage I Attraction Offer: Free Trial

> $0 then $399 per month after 30 days

Stage II & III Upsell + Continuity: Pay Less Now/Pay More Later + Lifetime Discount

> Pay $297 Now and Keep That Rate For Life

Author Note: I love this offer. It's nasty. It combines free trial, pay less now/pay more later, lifetime discount, and is an attraction offer, an upsell offer, and a continuity offer. A six-headed money-making monster. This is just a 'taste' of how creative you can get by combining these.

Dog Food (Physical Product)

Stage I Attraction Offer: Buy X Get Y Free

Buy Four Months of Food, Get Two Months Free

Stage II Upsell Offer: Classic Upsell *(like the rental car story)*

Do you want monthly→Dog toys?→Dog vitamins?

Stage II Downsell Offer: Feature Downsell

Just the premium food then? You don't want anything else do you?

Stage III Continuity Offer: Automatic Renewal after first bulk purchase.

After your six months, it continues month-to-month. Cancel anytime!

Make Your Own Money Model

Step 1) Start With An Attraction Offer. The goal is to turn strangers into customers and cover our costs. So, figure out what you're going to sell. Then, figure out the best way to present it. The Attraction Offer section has my top favorites: Win Your Money Back, Giveaways, Decoy Offers, Buy X Get Y Free, Pay Less Now or Pay More Later. Then, *advertise it*. If you get leads who turn into customers, you're on your way. Figuring out what works best may take up to a year. If you want to learn more about advertising, make sure to check out my second book *$100M Leads*.

Step 2) Pick An Upsell Offer. The goal is to get 30-day profits *well above* our costs of getting a new customer and delivering what you offer to them. Remember, once you solve a problem, another appears. Those problems also need solutions. You solve the problems your Attraction Offer creates with Upsell Offers. So pick the Upsell Offer that best matches the problem you solve and how you solve it. The Upsell Offer section gives you my four favorites: The Classic Upsell, Menu Upsell, Anchor Upsell, Rollover Upsell. Then, make your offer at their time of greatest need.

Step 3) Pick A Downsell Offer. The goal is to get customers who said no to your last offer to say yes to another offer. This way, you'll sell *way more people* than you otherwise would—so you make more total cash *from the same number of leads*. The Downsell Offer section shows you my three favorites. If you want to keep your price the same, *change how they pay* with Payment Plan Downsells or Trials. If you want to charge less, change *what they get* with Feature Downsells. And best of all, you can alternate between them in the same sale. The more flexible you make your offers, the more people will buy them.

Step 4) Pick A Continuity Offer. The goal here is to get one last sale in our 30-day window and stack recurring cash. So, I try to include continuity in business *eventually*. My three favorite Continuity Offers are: Continuity Bonuses, Continuity Discounts, and Waived Fee Offers.

Sometimes the best timing for Continuity Offers happens *after* the first thirty days, and that's OK. *It's better to make the offer at the right time than to try and force it at the wrong time.*

Author Note: Bootstrapped Businesses Must Get Customers At A Profit.

Unless you get outside investors...start with a fortune...or, have an endless source of free customers...achieving a *Money Model is the only way you can profitably scale*. Otherwise, you run out of cash and go out of business before you even have a chance.

Important Notes

Perfect One Offer At A Time. It's tempting to implement a whole Money Model at once. Don't. Stick to your stage. Pick one offer. Try it. Keep doing it until it works reliably. Then, after it's reliable, do it so many times it gets automatic. *Then*, go to the next stage.

Patience is still the fastest way to get to your goal. So you'll need to measure in quarters, not weeks. You either build it right or you build it again. And again. And again. Building again—no matter how fast—still takes longer than building it right the first time.

Raise Price In Stages. Make new offers cheap at first. Then, as you get yeses, raise the price. Lots of early yeses get customer feedback and make the product better. Then, as the offer gets reliable, start raising the price. And keep raising the price until you cannot make up for the nos with the extra cash you make from the yeses. In other words, keep raising the price until you make less money.

Simple Scales. Fancy Fails. Get as much as you can out of what you have. Remember, it's less about having 100 products to offer, and more about having 100 ways to offer your product. Think more ways to sell the same thing, not more things to sell. If I offer personal training, I can offer one, two, three, four etc. sessions per week. *This turns one product into many offers.*

IMPORTANT Affiliate Products Can Fill Money Model Gaps. An affiliate relationship just means you sell other peoples' stuff for a commission. If you don't have anything to offer, and want to start a business, you can offer somebody else's stuff. If you have a single offer, and want to add more offers to your Money Model, you can offer somebody else's stuff. If you have a $100M business, and want to make more money without adding the operational headache, you can offer somebody else's stuff. In short, you can always offer somebody else's stuff in your Money Model. Here are a few examples:

- Service: A dental agency sends their dentist clients to a braces manufacturer. The manufacturer sends them commissions for each dentist client they send. More money. No extra work. Voila.

- Local Business: A massage therapist sells their clients somebody else's home massage tools, exercise bands, medicine balls, etc. The customer pays through the therapist, and the other company ships it right to the customer. A few extra words. A lot of extra money. No extra service delivered.

- Digital Product: An educator tells his clients to use a specific customer service software. The software company sends the consultant a commission for every sign-up.

Turn Attraction Offers Into Continuity Offers With Automatic Renewal. This makes it a two-for-one. For example, if you do a Buy 6 Months Get 6 Months Free Offer, they can roll automatically into a month-to-month subscription at the end of 12 months. This gets the benefits of Attraction and Continuity Offers. A small tip with *big* implications.

You Can Mix And Match Offers However You Want. I present offers this way because that's how I use them. But if you recall, I learned many of them from people who used them differently than me! Many of these offers you can use *anywhere*. You can use Upsell tactics in your Attraction Offer. You can install a Downsell process with *every* offer. You can use a Continuity Offer to attract new customers. There are no rules. You can do whatever you want. I show you stuff one way, *but I fully expect you to use it in another*. So, start with the way I suggest it. Then, as you get better, experiment. It's how I learned this stuff. And it's how you'll learn it too.

Summary

- A Money Model is a deliberate sequence of offers.

- Money Models have three stages: Get Cash (Attraction Offers), Get More Cash (Upsells & Downsells), Get The Most Cash (Continuity Offers).

- To make your own Money Model, start with an Attraction Offer. Once it gets you customers and cash, add an Upsell Offer. From there, add Downsell Offers to get even more people to buy. Then, finally add in your Continuity Offer.

- Do not try and implement a full Money Model at once. It will break your business.

- Don't start more businesses just to make more offers. It's less about having 100 products to offer, and more about having 100 ways to offer your product.

- To sell more stuff without starting 100 businesses, offer stuff from *other* businesses and *let them deliver*.

- Affiliate Relationships can fill gaps in your Money Model without the headache of delivery.

- Price new offers low enough that you will get lots of yeses. Use customer feedback to improve your product. Then, start raising the price until you stop making more money.

- A *$100M Money Model* eliminates cash as a bottleneck for growth. Mission accomplished.

FREE GIFT: Make Your Own Money Model Step-By-Step Training

Whew. There's a lot in this chapter. It's also, arguably, the most important one in the book. So, to make sure you don't get stuck, I made you a video walking through this process step by step. As usual, you can watch it free (no opt-in needed) at acquisition. com/training/money. Or, you can scan the QR code.

Ten Years In Ten Minutes

The best thing a human can do is to help another human being know more. - Charlie Munger

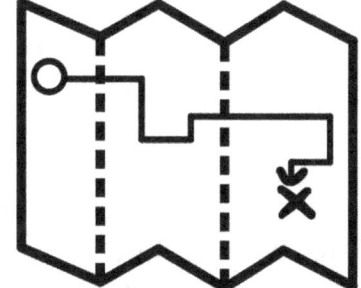

Where Money Models Fit In The Grand Scheme Of Things

My first book, *$100M Offers*, answered the question: *What should I sell?* Answer: an offer so good people feel stupid saying no. My second book, *$100M Leads*, answered the next natural question: *How do I find these people?* Answer: You advertise. This book, *$100M Money Models*, answers the next natural question: *How do I get them to buy it?* Answer: A Money Model.

What We Covered

We've covered a lot. And I think organizing what we learned into one place helps it sink in. So I made this "back of the napkin" list of what we've covered and why.

1) A **Money Model** is a series of offers designed to increase how many customers you get, how much they pay, and how fast they pay it.

2) **A good Money Model** *makes more profit from a customer than it costs to get and service them in the first 30 days.* That's the bare minimum.

3) **A $100M Money Model** *makes more profit from one customer than it costs to get and service many customers in the first 30 days,* which removes cash as a limiter to scaling your business.

4) Money Models have **four types of offers**: Attraction Offers, Upsell Offers, Downsell Offers, and Continuity Offers.

5) **Attraction Offers** get customers by offering something free or at a discount. Often, they also make money by offering a *better deal* at a higher price. We covered five.

   a) <u>Win Your Money Back</u>: *You* set a goal for the customer *and* tell them how to reach it. If they reach it, then they qualify to get their money back *or* get it back as store credit.

   b) <u>Giveaways</u>: You advertise a chance to win a big prize in exchange for contact information and anything else you want. After picking a winner, you offer everyone else the big prize at a discounted price.

   c) <u>Decoy Offers</u>: You advertise a free or discounted offer. When the lead asks to learn more, you *also* present a more valuable premium offer. The premium offer includes more features, benefits, bonuses, guarantees, and so on.

   d) <u>Buy X Get Y Free</u>: You offer customers free stuff in exchange for buying other stuff for money. The more free stuff and the higher its value, the more people buy.

   e) <u>Pay Less Now or Pay More Later</u>: You give people a choice to pay full-price later OR pay a discounted price now *and* get additional bonuses.

6) **Upsell Offers** are whatever you offer next. Typically, more, better, or newer versions of what they just bought. These get you more cash fast. We covered four.

   a) <u>The Classic Upsell</u>: You offer the solution to the customer's next problem the moment they become aware of it. *You can't have X without Y!*

   b) <u>Menu Upsells</u>: You tell customers which options they don't need. Then, tell them what they do need *and* how to get their value from it. *You don't need that…you need this.*

   c) <u>Anchor Upsells</u>: You offer your most expensive thing first. If the customer balks, you offer a much-cheaper-and-still-acceptable-alternative. *No worries. If you don't care about X, this may be a better fit for you.*

   d) <u>Rollover Upsells</u>: You credit some or all of a customer's previous purchases toward your next offer. *Since you already spent $500, I'll just credit that towards you staying a full year.*

7) **Downsell Offers** are whatever you offer after someone says no. And by turning Nos into Yeses you make more money. We covered three.

    a)   <u>Payment Plan Downsells</u>: You offer the same product at the same price, but they pay some now and the rest over time. *When do you get paid? Let's do half now and half then?*

    b)   <u>Trial With Penalty</u>: You let customers try your product or service for free *so long as they meet your terms.* If they do, they have a better chance of becoming paying customers. If they don't, they pay. *If you do X, Y, Z, I'll let you start for free.*

    c)   <u>Feature Downsells</u>: You lower prices by changing what the customer gets. I offer lower quantity, lower quality, lower price alternatives, or cut optional components entirely. *If you're okay without a guarantee, I can knock off $400.*

8) **Continuity Offers** provide ongoing value that customers make ongoing payments for—until they cancel. These boost the profit of every customer and give you one last thing to sell. We covered three.

    a)   <u>Continuity Bonus Offers</u>: You give the customer an awesome thing *if* they sign up today. Typically, the bonus itself has more value than the first continuity payment. *If you sign up today, you also get XYZ valuable thing.*

    b)   <u>Continuity Discount Offers</u>: You give the customer free time, now or later, *if* they sign up today.

    c)   <u>Waived Fee Offers</u>: First, you ask the customer to pay a startup fee as part of joining a month-to-month program. Then, you offer to discount the *entire* fee *if* they commit longer term. If they cancel inside the term, they pay the fee.

9) You build Money Models **one stage at a time**.

    a)   Once I get customers reliably *then* I make sure they pay for themselves reliably *then* I make sure they pay for other customers reliably *then* I start maximizing each customer's long-term value. *Then*, I print as much money as I can.

Bottom Line: The knowledge in these bullets brought me more free *and* profitable customers than I've known what to do with. If executed, they will do the same for you. And with that, cash will no longer constrain your business. I hope this book helps you grow your dream *as big as you darn well please.*

Also, since you are one of the few who actually finish what you start, I want to leave you with a parting gift: some closing remarks that got me through hard times.

    171

Final Thoughts

You don't become confident by shouting affirmations in the mirror: You become confident by giving yourself a stack of undeniable proof that you are who you say you are. Outwork your self-doubt.

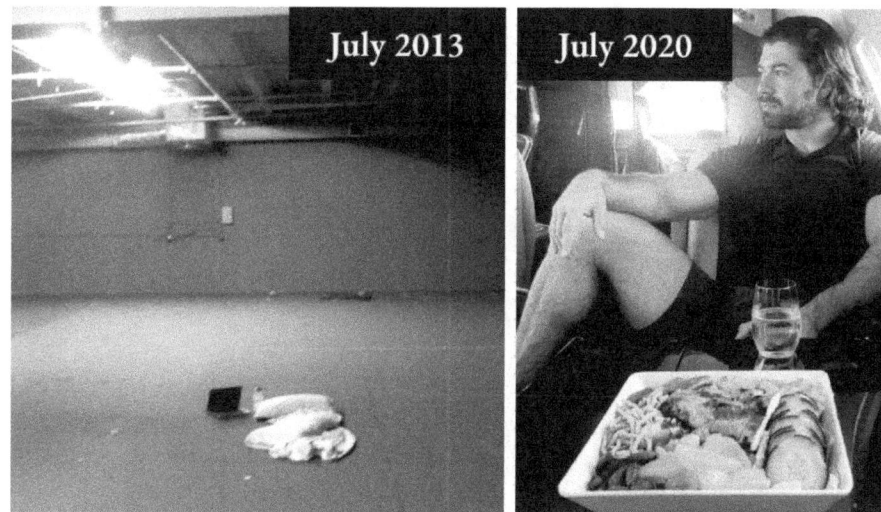

An actual post I made on July 25, 2020. *Before* I made my life public.

***

Leila snapped this when I wasn't looking and I was like "DAYUMM I look pensive AF" 😄

Anyways, this is the second time we've taken a private jet.

And...it was dope.

They figure if you go down with the ship, your seatbelt won't save you.

Regardless—to every entrepreneur who is disappointing their parents, wives, husbands, friends, fake friends, and everyone else who doubts you.

#1 I AM YOUR BIGGEST FAN.

#2 It's about to get real, so get hard fast.

#3 You cannot lose if you do not quit. I used to repeat that to myself over and over when I didn't want to keep doing it.

If you feel hopeless...welcome to entrepreneurship. If you feel like you'll never make it...you're on the right path. If you feel like you're a disappointment to everyone you know...Keep. Moving. Forward.

Because at the end of the rainbow isn't a pot of gold.

It's you.

The real you.

That's been underneath all along whispering in your ear—just one more step....one more call...one more sale.

When I say I'm your biggest fan, it's because I was there. And I know you because I know EXACTLY what that FEELS like. Having both 100% confidence and 1,000% doubt. At the same time. Here's all you gotta do:

Just keep moving.

Keep fighting.

Keep improving.

Your time will come.

Success is the only revenge.

***

So right now you might be where I was back when I started. Working in a concrete coffin, under blinding fluorescent lights, wanting to escape. You might be overwhelmed by all the stuff you have to do to succeed. But with that uncertainty, know that every entrepreneur, past and present, shoulders the burden with you. I've been there. They've been there. You are not alone. I share these stories as I experienced them so you can benefit from them as I have.

So here's my promise: follow the lessons, the money will come.

Be one of zero.

Alex Hormozi, Founder, Acquisition.com

PS - I've got some free goodies for you for finishing what you started.

Free Goodies

Nom nom nom.

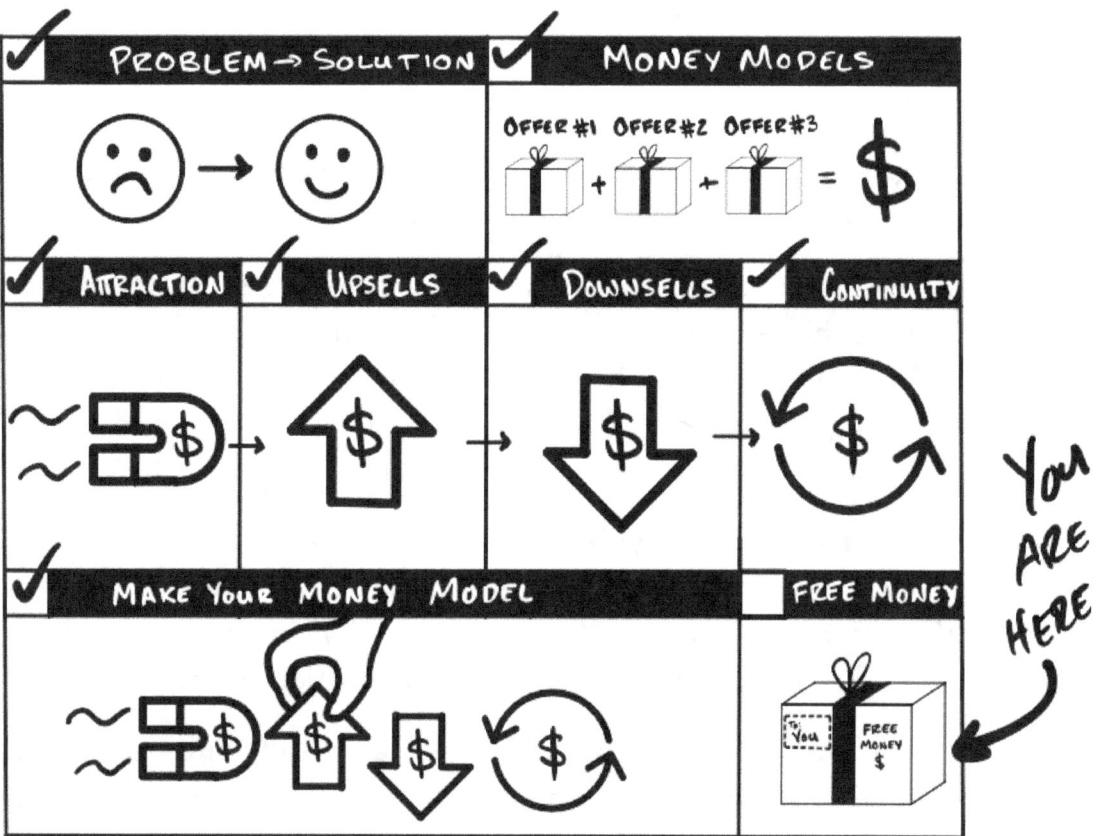

Kinda like the previews after the credits finish, if you're still with me, I wanted to give you a bunch of goodies.

1) **If you're struggling to figure out <u>who</u> to sell to**, I released a chapter called "Your First Avatar." You can get it for free at **Acquisition.com/avatar.** Just pop in your email and we'll send it over.

2) **If you're struggling to figure out <u>what</u> to sell**, you can go to Amazon or wherever you buy books and search "Alex Hormozi" and *$100M Offers*. It should get you on the right path.

3) **If you're struggling to <u>get people interested in</u> what you sell,** you can go to Amazon or wherever you buy books and search "Alex Hormozi" and *$100M Leads*. It should get you on the right path.

4) **If your company is over $1M in EBITDA (profit)**, we'd love to help you scale. It brings so much pleasure to know companies have grown much bigger and faster than mine *because they avoided the mistakes I made*. If you want us to take a look under the hood and see if we can help go to **Acquisition.com**.

5) **If you want a job at Acquisition.com** or in one of our companies—we love hiring from #mozination. Our best returns come from investing in great people. Go to **Acquisition.com/careers/open-jobs**, and you can see all the available openings.

6) To get the **free book downloads and video trainings** that come with this book, go to **Acquisition.com/training/money**.

7) **If you like listening to podcasts and want to hear more**, my podcast at the time of this writing is top 5 in entrepreneurship and top 15 in business in the US. You can get there by searching "Alex Hormozi" wherever you listen. Or, by going to **Acquisition.com/podcast**. I share useful and interesting stories, valuable lessons, and the essential mental models I rely on every day.

8) **If you like to watch videos**, we put a lot of resources into our free training, available for everyone. We intend on making it better than any paid stuff out there, and let you decide if we succeeded. You can find our videos on YouTube or wherever you watch videos by searching "Alex Hormozi."

9) **And if you like short-form videos**, check out the bite-sized content we pump out daily at **Acquisition.com/media**. You'll see all the places we post and you can pick the ones you like the most.

And last, thank you again. Please be one of those givers and **share this with other entrepreneurs by leaving a review**. It would mean the world to me. I'm sending you business-building vibes from my desk. I spend a lot of time there, so it's a lot of vibes. May your desire be greater than your obstacles.